O9-CFS-817

Twayne's English Authors Series

Sylvia E. Bowman, *Editor*

INDIANA UNIVERSITY

Thomas Sackville

165

Thomas Sackville

By NORMAND BERLIN

University of Massachusetts
Amherst

Twayne Publishers, Inc. :: New York

Library of Congress Cataloging in Publication Data

Berlin, Normand.
Thomas Sackville.

(Twayne's English authors series, TEAS 165)
Bibliography: p. 134
1. Dorset, Thomas Sackville, 1st Earl of, 1536-1608.
PR2499.D5Z57 821'.3 73-18407
ISBN 0-8057-1471-5

MANUFACTURED IN THE UNITED STATES OF AMERICA

To Adam and David

Preface

For Harry Levin, "the remarkable train of circumstance that made it possible for Shakespeare to write his plays is . . . the central epoch of literary history." Some may wish to disagree with Levin's choice of the central epoch — I do not — but none would deny that the train of circumstance was indeed remarkable. In the push of literary history toward the achievement of Shakespeare, Thomas Sackville plays an important part, one for which he has received the respectful admiration of students of literature. But this admiration has not taken the form of close discussion of his poems and play in order to increase their enjoyment. In fact, since Sackville's work is rarely discussed in terms that do not specifically relate to literary history, my purpose is to help correct this imbalance.

My study has two major aims — to examine closely Sackville's poems, the "Induction" and the *Complaint,* and his play, *Gorboduc,* as works of art, and to discuss the exact nature of Sackville's contribution to literary history. The heart of this book, Chapters 4 to 6, contains the critical commentaries on the poems and play. Chapter 1 presents those aspects of Sackville's life which shed light on his literary efforts. In Chapter 2, I detail the genesis of *The Mirror for Magistrates* and consider the part played by Sackville in the production of this important collection of tragical narratives. The sources of the "Induction" and the *Complaint* are discussed in Chapter 3 in an attempt to see clearly the Renaissance qualities of Sackville's mind and art. The last chapter evaluates Thomas Sackville's contribution to the development of Elizabethan tragedy.

As my notes and references indicate, I am indebted to the scholars and critics who have examined and interpreted the many and various aspects of Elizabethan literature. I would like to give special acknowledgment to Paul Bacquet and S. F. Johnson. The former produced an admirable biography and critical study of Thomas

Sackville; the latter has written an eminently publishable but unpublished Harvard University doctoral dissertation which contains a fine discussion of *Gorboduc*.

I wish to thank the officers and staffs of the Folger Shakespeare Library, the New York Public Library, and the University of Massachusetts Library for their facilities and assistance. I am grateful to the administration of the University of Massachusetts for a Faculty Growth Grant which gave me the opportunity to do the basic research for the book.

I thank Barnes and Noble, Inc. for permission to quote from *The Mirror for Magistrates,* ed. Lily B. Campbell (New York, 1960), and Houghton Mifflin Company for permission to quote from *Chief Pre-Shakespearean Dramas,* ed. J. Q. Adams (New York, 1924).

My deepest thanks belong to my wife Barbara, who has given me help and encouragement throughout and who has created the kind of atmosphere that makes possible the writing of a book.

Normand Berlin

The University of Massachusetts

Contents

Preface
Chronology
1. Sackville, the Statesman 13
2. *The Mirror for Magistrates* 24
3. A Renaissance Synthesis: The Sources of Sackville's Poems 32
4. The "Induction" 44
5. The *Complaint* 60
6. *Gorboduc* 80
7. Thomas Sackville and Elizabethan Tragedy 120
Notes and References 128
Selected Bibliography 134
Index 139

Chronology

1536 Thomas Sackville born at Buckhurst in the parish of Withyam, Sussex; the only son of Sir Richard Sackville, first cousin to Anne Boleyn, mother of Queen Elizabeth.

1551(?) Attends Oxford University; exact dates unknown.

1555 Marries Cicely Baker, daughter of Sir John Baker, a Privy Councillor. Admitted to Inner Temple, of which his father was governor, but does not take the degree of barrister.

1558 Sits as member of Parliament.

1561 *Gorboduc* produced on Jan. 6 at the Inner Temple and repeated on Jan. 18 for the Queen at Whitehall.

1563 Second edition of *The Mirror for Magistrates;* containing Sackville's "Induction" and *Complaint of Henry, Duke of Buckingham.* Returned again as member of Parliament.

1563-1566 In Italy and France on diplomatic business for the Queen.

1566 Sir Richard Sackville dies on April 21, thereby leaving his son in charge of a vast inheritance.

1567 Knighted on June 8. On the same day made a peer with the title Baron Buckhurst.

1570 The second and authorized edition of *Gorboduc* printed by John Day.

1571 Sent to France to congratulate Charles IX on his marriage to Elizabeth of Austria. Attempts to forward negotiations for the marriage of Queen Elizabeth to the Duke of Anjou. Granted an honorary degree of Master of Arts from Cambridge.

1572 Appointed commissioner at the state trial of Thomas Howard, Duke of Norfolk, who was accused of high treason for his communication with Mary, Queen of Scots.

1586 Execution of Mary, Queen of Scots, to whom, according to some sources, Sackville was sent to announce the sentence of death.

1587 Sent by the Queen to investigate the Low Countries, then under the governorship of the Earl of Leicester. Recalled because of alleged mismanagement a few months later and directed by the Queen to confine himself to his house, which he did for nine months.

1588 Restored to the Queen's favor on the death of Earl of Leicester.

1589 Elected Knight of the Garter.

1591 Appointed Lord Chancellor of Oxford University.

1599 Made Lord High Treasurer of England on May 15, succeeding Lord Burghley.

1601 Sits as Lord High Steward of England at the trial of the Earl of Essex.

1603 On the accession of James I, Sackville created Lord High Treasurer for life.

1604 Created Earl of Dorset on March 13.

1608 Sackville dies at the council table, Whitehall, on April 19. Solemnities of funeral performed in Westminster Abbey. Buried in the Sackville Chapel, adjoining the parish of Withyam.

CHAPTER 1

Sackville, the Statesman

THOMAS Sackville's literary fame rests on his youthful productions — the "Induction" to *The Mirror for Magistrates*, the *Complaint of Henry, Duke of Buckingham*, and the play *Gorboduc*. He left the writing of literature behind him when he assumed the burdens and honors of the life of a statesman. Much of his later life, therefore, is not altogether relevant to a discussion of Sackville the writer. Yet, these later years cannot be fully dismissed, because in Thomas Sackville we have an interesting example of a man's life that imitated art — of a statesman whose moral, religious, and political attitudes are already distinctly seen in his youthful writings. Thomas Sackville's life and art were of a piece; the youth was father of the man. An examination of selected aspects of the man's life helps us to understand more clearly the writings of the youth and also enables us to discern more sharply his individual voice.

I *Family and Education*

Devotion to his country and queen came to Thomas Sackville by birth. His ancestor, a Herbrand de Sackville, came to England with William the Conqueror; and from him through Sir Richard Sackville, Thomas's father, flowed the blood of generations of knights. Thomas Sackville and Queen Elizabeth had a common ancestor, Sir William Boleyn, whose daughter was Sackville's grandmother and whose son was the father of Anne Boleyn and the grandfather of Queen Elizabeth.

Sackville was born at Buckhurst in the parish of Withyam, Sussex, in 1536.[1] His father held important positions in the realm, including Chancellor of the Court of Augmentation to Edward VI and Mary and Under-Treasurer of the Exchequer to Queen Elizabeth. Although Sackville's early education is somewhat clouded in mystery, we can be reasonably sure that it was a good one; for his father displayed definite views on the importance of education in an interesting conversation recorded by Roger Ascham:

Sir Rich. Sackville came up sone after, and finding me in her Majesties privy chamber, he tooke me by the hand, and carying me to a windoe, said, 'M. *Ascham,* I would not for a good deal of monie have been, this day, absent from dinner. Where I said nothing, yet I gave as good eare, and do consider as well the taulke that passed, as anyone did there. M. Secretarie said very wisely, and most truely, that many yong wittes be driven to hate learninge before they know what learninge is. I can be good witnes to this myselfe: for a fond scholemaster, before I was fullie fourtene yeare olde, drave me so, with fear of beating, from all love of learninge, as nowe, when I know what difference it is to have learninge, and to have little, or none at all, I feel it my greatest griefe, and find it my greatest hurte, that ever came to me, that it was my so ill chance to light upon so lewde a scholemaster. But seeing it is but vain to lament thinges paste, and also wisdome to looke to thinges to come, surelie, God willing, if God lend me life, I will make this my mishap, some occasion of good hap to litle Robert Sackville, my sonnes sonne; for whose bringinge up I would gladlie, if it so please you, use speciallie your good advice. I heare say, you have a sonne much of his age: we will deale thus togither: Point you out a scholemaster, who, by your order, shall teache my sonne and yours, and for the rest I will provide, yea though they three do cost me a couple of hundred poundes by year; and besides you shall find me as fast a friend to you and yours, as perchance any you have.' Which promise the worthie Gentleman surelie kept with me untill his dying daye.[2]

Sir Richard was talking about his grandson, but we can assume that his own son had also been affected by his attitude. In all probability Thomas Sackville followed the ordinary course of studies at a grammar school; and, although there is no specific evidence recorded, he almost certainly studied at Oxford University. George Abbot's funeral sermon places Sackville at Oxford, and it quotes no less a personage than Queen Elizabeth about Sackville's ability as a student: "Her Highnesse was pleased to decipher out his life, by seven steps or degrees: the first was his younger daies, the time of his scholarship, when first in that famous Universitie of Oxford, and afterward in the Temple, . . . he gave tokens of such pregnancie, such studiousnesse and judgement, that he was held in no way inferiour to any of his time or standing."[3]

On July 1, 1555, Thomas Sackville was admitted to the Inner Temple; but it seems that he did not take the degree of barrister. Not to do so was usual for young men who wanted the education to pursue administrative duties but had no desire to practice law. The

Inner Temple is closely bound to Sackville's literary career, because it was there that *Gorboduc* was first performed in 1561; but Sackville had already written "The Induction" and the *Complaint.*

II *Courtier and Statesman*

From what we know or can asume about his education, Thomas Sackville was preparing himself to be a courtier and the head of a noble house. That he did not become a typical Renaissance courtier was probably the result of familial demands placed upon him as the young head of a household and by the political pressures that inevitably would cling to a man whose family was actively involved in politics and whose Queen happened to be a relative. His sonnet commending Sir Thomas Hoby's translation of Castiglione's *Courtier* indicates his interest in the concept of an ideal courtier:

Thomas Sackvylle in commendation of the
worke
To the Reader

These royal kinges, that reare up to the skye
Their palaice tops & decke them all with gold:
With rare and curious woorkes they feed the eye:
And showe what riches here great Princes hold.
A rarer work and richer far in worth,
Castilios hand presenteth her to the,
No proude, ne golden Court doth he set furth,
But what in Court a Courtier ought to be.
The prince he raiseth houge and mightie walles,
Castilio frames a wight of noble fame:
The kinge with gorgeous Tyssue claddes his halles,
The Court with golden vertue deckes the same,
Whos passing skill, lo Hobbies pen displaise
To Brittain folke, a work of worthy praise.[4]

He tried during his life to show "what in Court a Courtier ought to be," his "vertue" always exemplary. A contemporary remarked about Sackville's affairs at court that

> I finde not that he was in any way snared in the factions of the Court which were all his time strong, and in every man's note: the Howards and Cecills of the one part, and my Lord Essex, etc. on the other: for he held the staff of the treasury fast in his hand which made them, once in a year, to be beholden to him: and the truth is, as he was a wise man and a stout, he had no reason to be

> a partaker, for he stood sure in blood, and in grace, and was wholly intentive to the Queenes service, and such were his abilities, that she receiv'd assiduous proofes of his sufficiency and it hath been thought she might have more cunning Instruments, but none of a more strong Judgment, and confidence in his ways which are Symptomes of Magnanimitie, Whereunto methinks his motto hath something of reference, *Aut numquam tentes, aut perfice*. As though he would have charactered in a word the genius of his house, or express some what of a higher Inclinations, then lay within his compasse; that he was a Courtier is apparant, for he stood alwaies in her eye, and in her favour.[5]

Sackville's service to England officially began when he stood for Parliament in 1558. He was returned again in 1563, in which year he seems to have won the confidence of the Queen, who asked that he be in continual attendance on her. At about Christmas, 1563, however, we hear of Sackville in Rome; and the many speculations concerning his reasons for the trip range from a delicate diplomatic mission to the completion of his education by making the grand tour. Whatever the reason, Rome provided his first lesson in diplomacy.

Because he ran out of money or in some other way excited suspicion, Sackville was imprisoned in Rome. His friends in that city, concerned about this indignity to an important young man, presented a testimonial in his behalf.[6] Once his identity was established, he was treated as a distinguished visitor and was received by the Pope. Discovering that there were fewer differences between England and Rome than he had originally expected, he offered to mediate in England through his father. Rome agreed to have him begin negotiations in England; but, when about to set sail for England, he received letters from his father urging him to stay on the Continent. He proceeded to Paris, wrote to Rome from there, and asked that another representative go in his place. But this was impossible because two previous ambassadors to England had been refused admission. Thomas Sackville's first attempt at diplomacy resulted in failure,[7] and he never forgot its lesson — that, in order to attain success, power must reinforce intention.

His father's death in 1566 left Thomas, the only son, in charge of an enormous fortune. By the age of thirty, Thomas Sackville, already married and a father, assumed the responsibilities of the head of a vast estate, could look ahead to many years of service to his country, and already looked back on his career as a man of letters. It is doubtful if Sackville ever had the pain of making a choice between a life of letters and one of active statesmanship, since the latter seems always to have been foremost in his mind, and since the former often dealt with matters of state. Only a few men, specially endowed, are presented with such decisions. Some men can lead both lives — Sir Francis Bacon, for example. Perhaps Thomas Sackville could have done both, since he was engaged in public service while he was writing the "Induction", the *Complaint*, and *Gorboduc* — but he chose to devote all his energy and time to his country and Queen.

The facts concerning the rest of Sackville's life testify to his statesmanship and the recognition of his gifts. He was knighted by the Duke of Norfolk before the Queen on June 8, 1567, and became Lord Buckhurst on the same day. He joined the Privy Council and became Commissioner at state trials. He was elected Knight of the Garter in 1589, and two years later he was appointed Lord Chancellor of Oxford University. When supporting the Oxford appointment, the Queen said of Sackville: that "wee have found none every way in our opinion more capable thereof then the Lord Buckhurst one of the Lords of our privie councell, one whoe besydes his judgement and longe experience in our affairs hath also in our knowledge even from his childhoode been a continuall favourer and furtherer of learning."[8] After many important diplomatic missions, he became Lord High Treasurer of England, succeeding Lord Burghley; and the position became his for life on the accession of James I in 1603. He was created Earl of Dorset four years before his death in 1608.

Some aspects of his life, however, deserve close attention because they are of particular interest to the readers of his poems and play. In 1571, Sackville was in France, ostensibly to congratulate Charles IX on his marriage to Elizabeth of Austria, but really to forward negotiations about a possible marriage between Queen Elizabeth and the Duke of Anjou, Charles's brother. Sackville was certain, as were most of his contemporaries, that the future safety of England depended upon an assured succession. Ten years before, he had attempted to influence the Queen in this connection when he and Thomas Norton wrote *Gorboduc*. Now, as a statesman, he was doing in political action what he had suggested as a writer. He was entrusted to receive and convey messages between Queen Elizabeth and Charles IX and his mother, Catherine de Medicis.

Sackville was treated with dignity wherever he went, and he is reported to have conducted his affairs graciously, discreetly, and effectively. The Anjou-Elizabeth match was the most important aspect of Anglo-French diplomatic correspondence until January, 1572,[9] but nothing came of the negotiations. When Sackville returned to England, matters were left in the capable hands of Sir Francis Walsingham, the resident ambassador in Paris. A visit from the French ambassador to England again saw Sackville in charge of negotiations, but Sackville refused to return to France without definite instructions about the marriage, a condition stemming perhaps from his earlier Roman affair. Neither the effectiveness of his diplomacy in 1571 nor the effectiveness of his play ten years earlier was able to influence significantly Queen Elizabeth's decision not to marry.

Of course, the question of Queen Elizabeth's marriage was a delicate one throughout her reign; and her strength and subtlety were brilliantly displayed in her refusal to succumb to the demands of everyone around her. Her policy, as Winston Churchill points out, was "to spend her life in saving her people from such a commitment, and using her potential value as a match to divide a European Combination against her."[10] With the advantage of hindsight, we can say that Elizabeth was right and her advisors, including Sackville, wrong. But Sackville's diplomatic mission reinforces the image that we have of the Sackville who wrote *Gorboduc* — a man passionately concerned about the safety of his country who was not afraid to suggest to his Queen a course of action that would alleviate a possible danger to the realm.

Loyalty and devotion also prompted Sackville's behavior on his mission to the Netherlands in 1587, probably the most important political assignment of his long career. The Low Countries, under the governorship of the Queen's favorite, the Earl of Leicester, had become uneasy about their relationship with England. For reasons not specifically known, but easy to speculate about, Leicester suggested that Sackville be appointed to investigate the existing difficulties. According to Jacobus Swart, Leicester's motives were either to gain a delay or to secure a scapegoat.[11] Leicester obviously underestimated Sackville's ability, for Sackville did manage to smooth out some of the difficulties; and the voluminous correspondence connected with this affair puts Sackville in the most favorable light. Despite the fact that his mission was distrusted from the start, despite the long and many conferences and discussions and quarrels, despite the opposition of Leicester, and despite the court intrigue that surrounded the mission, Sackville, by means of wisdom and moral courage, was able to create an atmosphere of cooperation and trust. His reports on the condition of the soldiers who were not provided for reveal his characteristic sympathy:

And so the pore soldiors are like to perish. For whos relief I have wished sir Thomas Sherley to impress 20 wekely until some order may come from your lordship, which for Jesus sake hasten with al spede, and that such vittellers may be apointed as wil have a consciens not to make them selves rich with the famine of pore soldiors. And if Her Majesty send not mony, and that with al spede for the paiment of her pore soldiors, I am afraid to think what mischiefs and miseries are like to folow.

I humblie . . . beseche Your Majestie that you will please to send over with all possible spede suche money as may suffice to make a full paie unto the 12 of this next month . . . which shall not only redound to Your Highness's great proffit — sith the keping of Your Majesty's treasure in your coffers doth yelde no interest unto you — but also shal be a matter of muche honour to your Highness and . . . shall be the meane to preserve the lives of nombers of your faithfull subiectes, which otherwies must needes dailie perish, whose former miseries, through want of meate and monie to relieve them, being made knowne unto me here, dooth — I protest to God — so muche moove my soule with commiseration of that which is past, and so tremble my hart to thinke of the like to come againe — as I most humbly beseche Your Majesty, even for Jesus Christes sake, to have compassion of suche their lamentable estate passed and to send present monie to preserve them from the like hereafter.

The many and notable good havens here and the great nomber of ships and mairiners in theis places, with their impreinable townes, if they were in the hands of a potent prince, that wold defend them and lastlie the seate of this shore, so nere and opposite unto the land and coast of England, lo, the sight of theis dailie in mine eie, conioned with the depe enrooted malice of that your so mightie enimie, who seketh to regaine them — theis things entring continuallie into the thoughtes and meditacions of my harte, and thereby, how much it importeth both the saffetie of yourself and your estate, theis be they, which in the abundance of my love and dutie to Your Majesty doo enforce me thus ernestlie to speake, write and wepe unto your Highness, least, when the occasion yet offered shall ons be gon and past, this blessed meane of Your Majesty's defence by God's provident goodnes thus put into your hands, will then utterlie be lost, lo, never, never more to be had or recovered againe.[12]

Sackville respectfully, but fearlessly, objected to the Queen's misplaced parsimony and also indicated the mistakes of her favorite's administration.

At one point in Sackville's mission, when the Queen suggested that he approach the Low Countries on the matter of peace with Spain, he replied that this would be a mistake and spoil everything. But when she prevailed, he obeyed her orders faithfully and carefully. Because his talk of peace did indeed irritate the Netherlands, he was reprimanded by the Queen — even though he was explicitly following her commands. The historian J.A. Froude records what the Queen in her own hand wrote at the end of an official reprimand to him: "Oh, weigh deeplier the matter than with so shallow a judgment to spill the cause, impair my honour, and shame yourself. Use your wit, that once was supposed better than to lose a bargain for the handling."[13] Sackville was recalled, and Leicester returned to the Netherlands, saying that "Buckhurst hath marred all."

Although Sackville performed his duty faithfully and often brilliantly, he was banished from the court. The reward of his service was disgrace. His grief was great, and it stemmed primarily from the Queen's disappointment with him: "Becaus my hart doth best know, with what grete faith and dutie I have in this negotiation served Her Majesty, my greif is the greater to be thus deprived from the sight and presens of Her Majesty. That after so mainy cares, travels, sorowes and afflictions as in this servis I have suffred, I may yet at lencth receave the comfort of her prinsly face and presens."[14] He obeyed the Queen's order so literally that he remained in his own house throughout the nine months of banishment, seeing no one, not even his wife and children. He knew he had been mistreated, but his obedience did not waver. To Lord Burghley he wrote:

> Thus rolleth my fortune upon the wheel of sorrows and uncertainties, and my comfort still upon protractions, which is a most strange thing unto me, when I consider what herein I have merited, what heretofore my former service hath deserved, what I have always been and will be to her Majesty, and what withall even her Highness' self hath pleased to be evermore to me; yea, and I am sure, still is in her most gracious heart towards me; and last of all both what his lordship is, and what I am myself; and that all this notwithstanding, I should be thus disgraced for a private's man respect.[15]

The words succinctly reveal a man who had the greatest love for and loyalty to his Queen and who himself suffered briefly because of the turning of the same wheel of Fortune he had treated poetically in his younger years.[16]

This banishment was the only time in Sackville's career that he suffered from the great displeasure of the Queen. When Leicester died in 1588, Sackville was restored to the Queen's favor. He was asked to deal with the Netherlands in 1589 and again in 1596 and 1598. In fact, the Netherlands had constantly asked for his services because the country held the highest opinion of him. From 1588 on, the honors bestowed on Sackville were many and high.

The uncertainties of Fortune affected him personally only once, in the Netherlands affair; but he witnessed the turning of the wheel many times as a commissioner at state trials. He had as a young man written of the slipperiness of high position, of the fall of princes, in his contributions to *The Mirror for Magistrates.* Now, as a statesman, he was able not only to witness firsthand the fall of princes, but also to serve as a lawful instrument in their fall. Among the many men on whom he sat in judgment were Thomas, Duke of Norfolk; Anthony Babington; Philip, Earl of Arundel; and, the most notorious, Robert Devereux, Earl of Essex. Sackville pointed out to Essex the way in which he might have escaped the penalty of death, and in general conducted himself, according to Bacon, "with gravity and solemnity." Sackville had had previous official dealings with Essex when he spoke in the Star Chamber on Essex's handling of the Irish rebellion. A portion of his speech is enough to indicate Sackville's effectiveness as an orator.

> Nowe as concerning the first, that is the vile and villanous proceedings of those who by their scandalous and seditious libells doe accuse, and censure (at their wills and pleasures) all sortes of men, yea kings, kingdomes and commonwealths, and that which is most vniust and odious of all others, surely in some sort their owne sacred Prince and Soveraigne, and the faithfull servants and councell*ors* of the State: these vipers and secret libellors doe much more (in my opinion) deserue death then those that commit open rebellions against the state. For against such as discover them selues open rebells, Princes (with the help of their good subiects) doe speedilie arme themselues and easilie suppresse them. Against the sword and bullet there is an Armour of proofe, yea against the common shot there are bulwarkes and rampards; but against those secret libellors there is noe remedie, there is noe resistance, for euen the most innocent person and the greatest and iustest kinge stand subiect to their stinge. Soe, as for myne owne opinion, I protest, if there were a Parliament, I should more willinglie give my voice to establish a lawe of death against them, then against a theife or a murtherer.[17]

Here is a traditional idea expressed with color and vigor. In his speech he stated that he held the Earl of Essex to be "so honorable and soe just" that he would admit the faults of his conduct. Now, at the trial of Essex, Sackville, acting as High Steward of England, had to judge and condemn the man whose ambitions violated Sackville's conviction of the loyalty and devotion due to a Queen. The career of Essex is a classic example of the fickleness of Fortune, and Sackville's career touched Essex's at significant points.

A more dramatic example of Sackville's involvement with the fall of princes belongs to tradition.[18] In 1586, Sackville was nominated one of the commissioners for the trial of Mary Stuart. His name is not mentioned among the peers who met at Fotheringay Castle, nor is it among those who met in the Star Chamber at Westminster to condemn Mary to death; but he is supposedly the one who was chosen to announce the sentence of death to the Queen, because of his skill in diplomacy and his essential gentleness of character. He performed his painful duty so sympathetically that Mary gave him a wood carving of the Procession to Calvary, one which is still preserved in the chapel at Knole. Mary was traveling on her own road to Calvary, or so she believed; and when the statesman Sackville met her on the road, he was rewarded for the gentleness that he had displayed throughout his career. The fall of Mary makes vivid the precarious state of the high and the mighty, a condition that Sackville the young man had already effectively described in words. Once again, Sackville's art was being mirrored by events in Sackville's life.

Devotion to country, a quality which interested the young writer and ruled the older statesman, remained with Sackville until his death. As he advanced in years, his health became progressively poorer: he was subject to rheums and coughs; he had to flee from cold and moist air; he slept no more than three hours at night; he often lived with great pain. But his concern for his country's health was greater than that for his own. At times he avoided taking remedies for fear that they would interfere with his country's business. He died suddenly at the council table — and the place itself testified to Sackville's service to the realm to the very last.

Death as a condition of life — not merely as he became increasingly ill and not merely in connection with the fall of princes — was part of the fabric of Sackville's mind. He was a religious man,[19] whose "faith was agreeable unto the word of God, and according to the profession of the renowned Church of England."[20] In a very devout preamble to his will, Sackville thanks God for making him a *man,* not a beast, with a soul and reason, and especially "a Christianman," for now he can "depart and die in assurance and comfort of my soules and bodies salvation and resurrection." His belief in the transitoriness of life was expressed by him in these effective words:

. . . that is a Truthe infallible, suche as every Christian oughte not onlie perfectlye to knowe, and steadfastlie beleve, but also continually to meditate and think upon; Namely, That we are born to dye; that nothing in this Worlde ys more certeyn then Deathe, nothing more incerteyne then the Hower of Deathe, and that noe Creature livinge knoweth neither when, where, nor howe it shall please Almightie God to call hym out of this Mortal life, so as here we live every Hower, naye, every Instant, a thousande wayes subject to the suddayne Stroake of Deathe, which oughte to terrifie, teache and warne us to make ourselves readye.[21]

Although this passage was written at the end of his life, it expresses a sentiment similar to that in the eighth stanza of young Sackville's "Induction":

And sorowing I to see the sommer flowers,
The lively greene, the lusty leas forlorne,
The sturdy trees so shattered with the showers,
The fieldes so fade that floorisht so beforne,
It taught me wel all earthly thinges be borne
To dye the death, for nought long time may last.
The sommers beauty yeeldes to winters blast.

That we are born to die is a truth infallible. In his pilgrimage from birth to death, Sackville served his country in difficult and exciting times with unswerving devotion. On the way, he also managed to make an important and lasting contribution to his country's literature.

CHAPTER 2

The Mirror for Magistrates

SACKVILLE the poet was as appreciated in his lifetime as Sackville the statesman. He received enthusiastic praise from many of his contemporaries. George Turberville said that Sackville was far worthier to translate Lucan than he, for Sackville had "a stately stile, a peerless pen" and was the best "in Brutus land."[1] Thomas Campion, dedicating his *Observations in the Art of English Poesie* to Sackville, called him "the noblest judge of Poesy, and the most honorable protector of all industrious learning."[2] Joshua Sylvester, dedicating to Sackville part of his translation of the *Divine Weeks* of Du Bartas, presented this sonnet to him:

> Not without Error, and apparent Wrong
> To thee; the Muses, and myself (the most)
> Could I omit, amid the Noble Host
> Of Learned Friends to Learning, and our song,
> To muster Thee; Thee that has lov'd so long
> The sacred Sisters, & (sad-sweetly-most)
> Thy Selfe hast sung (under a fayned Ghost)
> The tragick Falls of our Ambitious Throng.
> Therefore, in honor of Thy younger Art,
> And of the Muses, honour'd by the same,
> And to express my Thankfull thoughts (in part)
> This Tract a sacre unto Sackvil's Name
> No les renowned for Numbers of Thine Owne,
> Than for thy love to Other's Labours showin.[3]

And Edmund Spenser, for whom Sackville was an important inspiration, praised Sackville in this dedicatory stanza of *The Faerie Queene:*

> In vain I thinke right honourable Lord,
> By this rude rime to memorize thy name;

> Whose learned Muse hath writ her owne record,
> In golden verse, worthy immortal fame:
> Thou much more fit (were leasure to the same)
> Thy gracious Soverains praises to compile,
> And her imperiall Maiestie to frame,
> In loftie numbers and heroicke stile.
> But sith thou maist not so, give leave a while
> To baser wit his power therein to spend,
> Whose grosse defaults thy daintie pen may file,
> And unadvised oversights amend.
> But evermore vouchsafe it to maintaine
> Against vile Zoilus backbitings vaine.[4]

Sackville, in fact, was probably Spenser's model for Aetion in *Colin Clouts Come Home Againe:*

> And there though last not least is *Aetion,*
> A gentler shepheard may no where be found:
> Whose *Muse* full of high thoughts invention,
> Doth like himselfe Heroically sound.

Praise for Sackville the poet did not stop, however, with his contemporaries. Scholars and critics of the late nineteenth and early twentieth centuries, including the influential Thomas Warton, heaped praise on him; but the most notorious was George Saintsbury's assertion, repeated often, that "his contributions to the *Mirror for Magistrates* contain the best poetry written in the English language between Chaucer and Spenser."[5]

I *Plan and Purpose*

All of these laudatory comments and poems are presented in connection with Sackville's contributions to one of the most important books of the sixteenth century, *The Mirror for Magistrates,* a collection of tragical narratives recited by the ghosts of famous men in British history. The earliest of the poetical histories published in the Elizabethan age, its plan was taken directly from John Lydgate's *The Fall of Princes,* which in turn had followed the model of Boccaccio's *De Casibus Virorum Illustrium.* In fact, originally, the *Mirror* was to have been bound in one volume with the *Fall of Princes.* The details of its origin, rather complicated ones, have been examined admirably by Professor Lily B. Campbell.[6]

Because the moral Lydgate was held in high esteem in Tudor

times, it was natural that a printer would attempt to publish his very popular *Fall of Princes.* John Wayland, the Queen's printer, had proposed before 1555 to reprint Lydgate's work — a series of verse tragedies in which the sins of the fallen are specifically explained — and to continue Lydgate's series by including "the chefe Prynces of thys Iland, penned by the best clearkes in such kind of matters that be thys day lyving." Wayland went with this project to William Baldwin — who was a printer, playwright, philosopher, and poet — but Baldwin said he would do it only with the help of other men. The printer secured the cooperation of seven men who met to consider the project. Baldwin's address to the reader explains that because both Boccaccio and Lydgate were dead, Baldwin should "usurpe Bochas rowme" — Boccaccio had acted as commentator and interlocutor in his *De Casibus* — and should become the interlocutor to whom the wretched English princes might make their complaints. The seven decided to begin where Lydgate left off, which was at the end of King Edward III's reign; and the various authors were to rely on the available English chronicles, especially those of Edward Hall, but also those of Robert Fabyan and Sir Thomas More.

The work of these authors was partly printed in 1555, but it was "stayed" by Queen Mary's chancellor, Stephen Gardiner, who probably saw in the historical narratives disturbing parallels to contemporary conditions; for these were anxious and dangerous days in the history of England. The book was not published until the first year of Queen Elizabeth's reign, 1559; it became one of the most popular books of the Elizabethan period, going through many editions. The 1559 edition contains nineteen tragedies and covers the historical period from Richard II to Edward IV. The edition of 1563 adds eight stories, and primarily concerns the reign of Richard III; it is also notable because it contains Sackville's "Induction" and *Complaint.* In 1574, John Higgins published a series of tragical narratives recounting the falls of "the first infortunate Princes of this lande: From the coming of Brute to the incarnation of our saviour and redemer Jesu Christ." In 1578, Thomas Blenerhasset issued a second series from Caesar to William the Conqueror. Whereas Baldwin and company kept within the limits of Hall's *Chronicle,* Higgins and Blenerhasset go outside it for their material. However, Higgins' series and Baldwin's were put together in 1587 and became the standard edition. The various editions testify to the discovery by the Elizabethans of the potentialities of British history for tragical narratives. Because it filled a need, the *Mirror,* as

Willard Farnham suggests, "eventually manifested a reproductive life of its own."[7]

The purpose of *The Mirror for Magistrates* is explained in Baldwin's address "to the nobilitye and all other in office," in which he states that magistrates bear "Gods owne office."

What a fowle shame wer it for any now to take vpon them the name and office of God, and in their doinges to shew them selves divyls? God can not of Iustice, but plage such shameles presumption and hipocrisy, and that with shamefull death, diseases, or infamy. Howe he hath plaged euill rulers from time to time, in other nacions, you may see gathered in Boccas booke intituled the fall of Princes, translated into Englishe by Lydgate: Howe he hath delt with sum of our countreymen your auncestors for sundrye vices not yet left, this booke named *A Myrrour for Magistrates,* can shewe: which therfore I humbly offre vnto your honors, beseching you to accept it fauorably. For here as in a loking glass, you shall see (if any vice be in you) howe the like hath bene punished in other heretofore, whereby admonished, I trust it will be a good occasion to move you to the soner amendment. This is the chiefest ende, whye it is set furth, which God graunt it may attayne.

In his address "to the reader" he continues to emphasize the moral purpose of the work, stating that he was asked by the printer to present, from where Boccaccio left off, the accounts of those with whom "Fortune had dalyed with here in this ylande: whiche might be as a myrrour for al men as well noble as others, to shewe the slyppery deceytes of the waueryng lady, and the due rewarde of all kinde of vices."

These statements by Baldwin — the Baldwin, incidentally, whose *Treatise of Morall Philosophy* (1547) continued to be a popular book in England — indicate the importance of the didactic element in the work. The purpose of the writers of the narratives was to teach the lessons of history; and the tragedies were selected, it seems, for their ability to demonstrate that punishment is related to sin.[8] Some of the titles to individual tragedies are: "Howe kyng Richarde the second was for his evyll governaunce deposed from his seat, and miserably murdered in prison." "How king James the first fro breaking his othes and bondes, was by gods suffrauns miserably murdred of his owne subiectes." "How Iacke Cade traiterously rebelling agaynst his King, was for his treasons and cruell doinges wurthely punyshed." "The infamous ende of Lord Ian Tiptoft Earle of Wurcester, for cruelly executing his princes butcherly commaundementes." The stories were meant to put the fear of God into the hearts of tyrants and to display the terrible consequences of their misrule.

The Mirror for Magistrates is exactly what its title indicates — a mirror, a glass, a reflection of the workings of Fortune and God's justice on the famous men of England's past. Presented for the benefit of each reader, but especially for magistrates, all were to *learn* by looking at the reflection. The hope of the writers, as of most Renaissance writers of moral history, was that a mirror reflecting the fall of princes would also reflect the man looking at the mirror. The mirror, ultimately, should allow a man to know himself — *Nosce teipsum.*

II *Sackville's Contributions*

Although Sackville's association with the group of men who planned the *Mirror* is clearly set down by Baldwin, the temptation has been great to attribute to Sackville a greater role than he actually played in the conception of this important work. Since his is the most well-known name among the writers of the *Mirror,* it is understandable that claims would have been made for him that cannot be supported by fact. But we have Baldwin's words, presented immediately before Sackville's "Induction":

> I have here the duke of Buckingham, king Richardes chyefe instrument, wrytten by mayster Thomas Sackuille. Read it we pray you sayd they: with a good wyl (quoth I) which is thys: After that he vnderstoode that some of the counsayle would not suffer the booke to be printed in suche order as we had agreed and determined, he purposed with him selfe to haue gotten at my handes, al the tragedies that were before the duke of Buckinghams, Which he would haue preserued in one volume. And from that time backeward euen to the time of William the conquerour, he determined to continue and perfect all the story him selfe, in such order as Lydgate (folowing Bocchas) had already vsed. And therfore to make a meete induction into the matter, he deuised this poesye: which in my iudgement is so wel penned, that I woulde not haue any verse therof left out of our volume. Nowe that you knowe the cause and meanyng of his doing, you shal also heare what he hath done. His Induccion beginneth thus.

The statement seems clear enough: Sackville suggested a plan whereby the editors could present the *Mirror* without censure. He may have hoped, as Swart speculates, to get the revised poem licensed because of the new chronology or because of his own good connections. In any case, the impression arose that Sackville was the creator of the original design of the *Mirror;* for Richard Niccols, in his preface to the 1610 edition, makes this statement:

> This worthie President of learning, intending to perfect all this storie himselfe from the Conquest, being called to a more serious expence of his time in the great State-affaires of his most royall Ladie and Soueraigne, left the dispose thereof to M. *Baldwine,* M. *Ferrers* and others, the composers of these Tragedies, who continuing their methode which was by way of dialogue or interlocution betwixt euery Tragedie, gaue it onely place before the Duke of *Buckinghams* complaint, which order I since hauing altered, haue placed the Induction in the beginning, with euery Tragedie following according to succession and the iust computation of time, which before was not obserued.

This account began the false tradition that Sackville was the primary inspiration of the *Mirror;* and it led to a rash of similar statements, the most influential of which was that of Thomas Warton:

> More writers than one were concerned in the execution of this piece: but its primary inventor, and most distinguished contributor, was Thomas Sackville the first lord Buckhurst, and first earl of Dorset. . . . About the year 1557, he formed the plan of a poem, in which all the illustrious but unfortunate characters of the English history, from the conquest to the end of the fourteenth century, were to pass in review before the poet, who descends like Dante into the infernal region, and is conducted by SORROW. Although a descent into hell had been suggested by other poets, the application of such a fiction to the present design, is a conspicuous proof of genius and even of invention. Every personage was to recite his own misfortunes in a separate soliloquy. But Sackville had leisure only to finish a poetical preface called an INDUCTION, and one legend, which is the life of Henry Stafford duke of Buckingham. Relinquishing therefore the design abruptly, and hastily adapting the close of his INDUCTION to the appearance of Buckingham, the only story he had yet written, and which was to have been the last in his series, he recommended the completion of the whole to Richard Baldwyne and George Ferrers.[9]

Among the others who present this view are R. W. Sackville-West, Sidney Lee in the *Dictionary of National Biography,* and V. M. Sackville-West. Joseph Haslewood,[10] in the important edition of the *Mirror* before Campbell's, demonstrated the falsity of the theory in 1815; and he has been upheld by later scholars — W. J. Courthope,[11] J. W. Cunliffe,[12] Marguerite Hearsey, Lily B. Campbell, and Paul Bacquet.

There is no reason to doubt Baldwin's statement that Sackville was planning to write more tragedies than the only one he presented, for the length of the "Induction" strongly suggests that it is introducing more than one tragedy. There are other indications as well. The Ghost of Henry is announced in this way: "Then first came Henry Duke of Buckingham." The word "first" obviously points to more tragedies to come. Also, when the Ghost addresses Sackville, he says: "And Sackeuylle sith in purpose nowe thou hast/ The woful fal of prynces to discryve." The plural "princes," reinforced by Baldwin's use of the word in the prose link after Sackville's poem, clearly indicates Sackville's intentions. Marguerite Hearsey's discovery of the manuscript which contains the "Induction" and the *Complaint* written as one poem adds complications to the theory but does not change it.

We are safe in assuming that Sackville did undertake to carry out his plan, but that he was side-tracked after completing only the "Induction" and the *Complaint*. Perhaps he was diverted by the writing of *Gorboduc* or by the affairs of the state. Whatever the reason, he abandoned his proposed, huge labor. The exact dates for the writing of the "Induction" and the *Complaint* have been the subjects of scholarly debates that have produced interesting insights into the history and editing of *The Mirror for Magistrates* as well as into Sackville's literary activity. Much of this discussion is outside the scope of this book, but it is important to place, even if only approximately, the writing of these poems within Sackville's short-lived literary career.

The "Induction" and the *Complaint* have come to us in two forms — as separate and continuous pieces in the 1563 edition of the *Mirror,* and as a single poem entitled *The Complaint of Henry, Duke of Buckingham* in the autograph manuscript found in St. John's College, Cambridge, which contains, in addition, an incomplete draft epilogue not found in the *Mirror*. This manuscript was discovered by Marguerite Hearsey; and, according to Hearsey, the poems were written immediately after the publication of *Tottel's Miscellany* in June, 1557, because of probable allusions to Surrey's poems found in that collection. She also states that the autograph copy is perhaps the copy used by the printer. However, Lily B. Campbell places the date of composition at 1555, whereas W. F. Trench, who wrote the first study of the history of the printing of the *Mirror,*[13] argues for 1554. Fitzroy Pyle, who presents the interesting suggestion that Baldwin himself edited Sackville's manuscript,[14] favors 1554, as does Swart, who supports his view with a detailed discussion of the four astronomical stanzas in the "Induction."[15]

The most thorough discussion of the dating is found, however, in Paul Bacquet's study. He admits that nothing permits us to date Sackville's poems precisely but that external and internal evidence points to a reasonable speculation that both poems were written before the 1559 edition was published. They were not included in that edition because the tragedies were arranged according to chronological order in history, beginning with Richard II and going through Edward IV, so that Buckingham did not belong to this group. It is probable, as Bacquet suggests, that the editor reserved the *Complaint* — and with it the "Induction," which he would not leave out ("I woulde not have any verse therof left out our volume.") — for a later edition.

By way of summary, as we look at the progress of events in connection with Sackville's contributions to *The Mirror for Magistrates,* we can be reasonably sure that the following sequence occurred. After an early attempt to print the *Mirror* in Queen Mary's reign had failed, Sackville had hoped to help Baldwin by planning an alternative publication and by writing a number of tragedies. The *Complaint* was probably written before the ban in Mary's reign, and the "Induction" written after Sackville's proposal to Baldwin of a new scheme, since the "Induction" is intended as a general introduction. Since the *Complaint* could not fit into the chronological scheme of the 1559 edition of the *Mirror* it was saved for a future edition and appeared in the 1563 edition with the "Induction," a poem too good to be denied publication.

We are on shakier ground when we try to speculate about the incomplete epilogue in the St. John's manuscript. Perhaps Sackville intended, after letting the poem lie about for a time, to publish the "'Induction" and the *Complaint* separately, thereby rounding out the one poem with a balanced epilogue. But he left the task unfinished, and the poems were eventually published in the 1563 edition. The exact date of the epilogue is unknown.[16] We can be certain, however, that both the "Induction" and the *Complaint* were written before Sackville's other literary effort, *Gorboduc;* and with these poems, we must begin a discussion of Sackville the poet.

CHAPTER 3

A Renaissance Synthesis: The Sources of Sackville's Poems

IN the unfinished epilogue to the *Complaint*, Sackville gives high praise to Virgil, Ovid, Chaucer, Wyatt, Surrey, Boccaccio, and Seneca. This combination is a characteristic Tudor one of the Classical, Medieval, and contemporary. The names indicate the sources of Sackville's borrowings and reaffirm that he was a man of his time. Like other writers of the sixteenth century, he read widely and borrowed freely, and his attitude toward borrowing was that of the Renaissance, which not only applauded the process of using the ideas and forms of the past but also asserted the necessity of imitation.

Imitation, of course, is not plagiarism in the modern sense. In fact, Englishmen had no word "plagiarism" until the beginning of the seventeenth century.[1] The Renaissance writer did not search for novelty; he attempted to transform and re-express what was said before. Renaissance learned culture was, as Hardin Craig asserts,[2] aggregative in its practices; and Craig regards the student's commonplace book as a paradigm of the kind of aggregative practice we find in most Renaissance writers. It was the center of the school course and is "the symbol of the learned mind of the Renaissance both in its habits and its objectives." A natural outgrowth of this aggregative habit was the demand for compilations in book form of selected quotations from the authors of the past; and the first book printed in English, *The Dictes or Sayings of the Philosophers,* was such a compilation.

Collecting, borrowing, and imitating, however, did not preclude originality. The Renaissance mind was not merely docile; it was aspiring. It used its sources in such a way that the new rendering of an old subject or the modern application of an old form produced something which could rival the original, which could bear the stamp of its own individuality. However, because borrowing was so extensive and pervasive, because imitation was an accepted practice, and because debts to older writers were so obviously part of a writer's output that acknowledgment was unnecessary, it is difficult to measure with exactness the extent or the nature of one writer's "influence" on another. Difficult, too, to determine whether one writer went directly to another writer or to a commonplace book or compilation of sayings. These difficulties bear directly on a discussion of Sackville's sources in the "Induction" and in the *Complaint*. I shall tread warily, even on ground that has already been paved.[3] My purpose is to indicate briefly and in a general way the kinds of borrowings we find in Sackville's poems.

I *The* "Induction"

An examination of the sources of the "Induction" must avoid the danger of attaching particular importance to the commonplaces of the period — clichés, conventional metaphors, and common themes. Many ideas found in Sackville are common both to the Middle Ages and to Classical antiquity. The theme of Fortune, for example, can be found in Seneca and Chaucer and Boethius, to name only three; from what source *exactly* Sackville may have derived his notion of fortune cannot be determined. So too the references to the fall of Troy, other mythological allusions, and examples from popular history are part of the public domain: they belong to a general Classical and Medieval heritage. To attribute Sackville's tone at a specific point in the poem to a particular source is also difficult and dangerous because the Renaissance appreciated most those ancient and Medieval works which were didactic, serious, and somber.

Keeping this caveat in mind, and realizing at the same time that Sackville is not an historical scholar collating authorities, checking sources, and methodically amalgamating, but a busy young man trying his poetic wings, we can investigate the more definite borrowings in the "Induction".

The most important of Sackville's Classical sources is Virgil. Swart goes so far as to say that the "Induction" is a paraphrase of Virgil,[4] and Elizabeth Nitchie considers it "the most elaborate piece of Virgilian imitation before Spenser."[5] Virgil had already been translated, but no English writer had attempted the kind of adaptation that Sackville achieved.

After the introductory stanzas, which are essentially Medieval in character, the poet meets Sorrow, who proposes to conduct him to the underworld; and here the borrowing from Virgil begins. The descent to Hell of Sackville and his guide is modeled after Aeneas' descent with the Sibyl. Similarities between passages are many, and suggestions in Virgil are fully exploited by Sackville. The following description of Lake Averne is an obvious example of direct borrowing from Virgil:

> An hydeous hole al vaste, withouten shape,
> Of endles depth, orewhelmde with ragged stone,
> Wyth ougly mouth, and grisly Iawes doth gape,
> And to our sight confounds it selfe in one.
> Here entred we, and yeding forth, anone
> An horrible lothly lake we might discerne
> As blacke as pitche, that cleped is Auerne.
>
> A deadly gulfe where nought but rubbishe growes,
> With fowle blacke swelth in thickned lumpes that lyes,
> Which vp in the ayer such stinking vapors throwes
> That ouer there, may flye no fowle but dyes,
> Choakt with the pestilent sauours that aryse.
> (204-15)

The passage in Virgil reads:

> His actis propere exsequitur praecepta Sibyllae.
> spelunca alta fuit vastoque immanis hiatu,
> scrupea, tuta lacu nigro nemorumque tenebris,
> quam super haud ullae poterant impune volantes
> tendere iter pinnis: talis sese halitus atris
> faucibus effundens supera ad convexa ferebat:
> unde locum Grai dixerunt nomine Aornon.
> (*Aeniad,* VI, 236-42)

The allegorical figures seen by Sackville at the entrance of Hell — Remorse, Dread, Revenge, Miserie, Care, Sleep, Old Age, Maladie, Famine, Death, War — are Virgil's figures; but Virgil gives each a line or less, whereas Sackville gives them thirty-six stanzas. For example, Virgil's "Palentesque habitant Morbi" becomes:

> And fast by him pale Maladie was plaste,
> Sore sicke in bed, her colour al forgone,
> Bereft of stomake, sauor, and of taste,
> Ne could she broke no meat but brothes alone.
> Her breath corrupt, her kepers euery one

Abhorring her, her sickenes past recure,
Detesting phisicke, and all phisickes cure.
(337-43)

The shield of Virgil's Aeneas points directly to Sackville's shield of war. The account of the fall of Troy, although a common story, has strong Virgilian echoes in its description of Cassandra's capture and Priam's death. The encounters with Charon and Cerberus owe much to Virgil's narrative.

In the main, Sackville telescopes Virgil's action and expands Virgil's words and suggestions into complete descriptions, often stressing minute details. Sackville, a keen student of Virgil, used the Latin text; but he was also indebted to Gawain Douglas's complete translation of the *Aeneid* (printed 1553) and, less so, to Surrey's translation of Books II and IV (1557). Part of Sackville's description of Averne, quoted above, could have come from Douglas's rendition of Virgil's lines.

Thar stud a dirk and profound cave fast by
Ane hiddouis hole, deip gapand and grisly
All full of craggis and of their sherp flint stanis
Quhilk wes weill dekkit and closit for the nanis
With a foull laik, als black as ony craw
. . . .
Quhairfor Grekis Avernus clepis this steid.[6]

This passage is so close to both Virgil and Sackville that it indicates the difficulty of attributing passages to specific sources.

Other classical borrowings can be found in the "Induction." Sackville goes to Seneca for some passages, the best of which comes from *Hercules Furens* and is the probable origin for one of Sackville's most effective stanzas:[7]

tuque, o domitur Somne malorum
requies animi,
pars humanae melior vitae,
volucre o matris genus Astraeae,
frater durae languide Mortis,
veris miscens falsa, futuri
certus et idem pessimus auctor,
pater o rerum, portus vitae,
lucis requies noctisque comes,
qui par regi famuloque venis,

pavidum leti genus humanum
cogis longam discere noctem.
(1066-77)

Sackville's paraphrase of the above is the second of the following stanzas on sleep:

By him lay Heauy slepe the cosin of death
Flat on the ground, and stil as any stone,
A very corps, save yelding forth a breath.
Small kepe tooke he whom Fortune frowned on.
Or whom she lifted up into the trone
Of high renowne, but as a liuing death,
So dead alyve, of lyef he drewe the breath.

The bodyes rest, the quyete of the hart,
The travayles ease, the still nightes feer was he.
And of our life in earth the better parte,
Reuer of sight, and yet in whom we see
Thinges oft that tide, and ofte that neuer bee.
Without respect esteming equally
Kyng Cresus pompe, and Irus pouertie.
(281-94)

Less frequently, the "Induction" contains borrowings from Plutarch and Valerius Maximus, but the latter is more important in the *Complaint.* Ovid, the Classical writer who had the greatest general appeal to the Renaissance, is missing from the "Induction." Undoubtedly the sophisticated poet of love, who is praised by Sackville in the epilogue, could find no place in a philosophical melancholy poem.

Besides going to the Classics for his borrowings, Sackville went to the other fountainhead of the Renaissance heritage, the Middle Ages, and especially to Chaucer and Lydgate. Sackville knew Chaucer's work and considered Chaucer "cheif that wrot in english vers/ above the best that ever brittain bred" (Epilogue, 15-16). The opening stanzas of the "Induction," giving the astronomical setting and describing the season, is Medieval in character and is reminiscent of many of Chaucer's introductions. Sackville's guide Sorrow, modeled after Virgil's Sibyl, as mentioned before, is also very close to Chaucer's guides, for she is pathetic and directly relevant to the poem's theme. Chaucerian passages are echoed throughout, but once again it is difficult to be sure that the direct source is Chaucer, or a Chaucerian imitator, or that the passage belongs to a general literary tradition. In the second stanza of "Induction," for example, we find "smale fowles flocking in their song." Now birds sing throughout Chaucer's poetry, as they do in Lydgate and others; in fact, English poetry is filled with singing birds. It is unrewarding, therefore, to attribute such a phrase directly to Chaucer.

However, other elements of the poem allow us to stand on firmer ground. For example, in describing Sorrow, Sackville writes: "her forceles handes together oft she smote/ . . . that in my dome was never man did se/ a wight not half so wobegon as she." Chaucer, in *The Romaunt of the Rose,* uses these words as part of a description of his Sorowe:

> So wo-begon a thyng was she.
> She al to dassht herself for woo,
> And smot togyder her hondes two.
> (336-38)

The connection here is tight; the Chaucerian inspiration is probable.

Sackville also owes a considerable debt to Lydgate and a smaller one to his contemporaries. It would be surprising if Sackville did not turn often to Lydgate since the *Fall of Princes* was the important model for *The Mirror for Magistrates.* For his examples from the lives of famous men of Greece and Rome, found in stanzas 58-62 of the "Induction," Sackville seems to have gone directly to Lydgate. And phrases from the *Fall of Princes,* the *Siege of Thebes,* and the *Complaint of the Black Knight* are spotted throughout Sackville's poems. Of his immediate predecessors among the English poets Sackville singles out Wyatt and Surrey in his epilogue, but he goes only to Surrey for occasional phrases from his translation of the *Aeniad* and from *A Plea for Mercy.*

These, then, are the important sources of Sackville's borrowings in the "Induction" — Virgil, Seneca, Chaucer, Lydgate, Douglas, Surrey. They are blended together in masterful fashion and become what is essentially Sackville's own. One passage, Sackville's description of Olde Age, can serve as an illustration of Sackville's ability to amalgamate the Classical and the Medieval, and can illustrate at the same time the difficulty in ascribing a specific passage to one particular source:

> And next in order sad Olde age we found
> His beard al hoare, his iyes hollow and blynde,

With drouping chere still poring on the ground,
As on the place where nature him assinde
To rest, when that the sisters had vntwynde
His vitall threde, and ended with theyr knyfe
The fleting course of fast declining life.

There heard we him with broken and hollow playnt
Rewe with him selfe his ende approching fast,
And all for nought his wretched minde torment.
With swete remembraunce of his pleasures past,
And freshe delites of lusty youth forwaste.
Recounting which, how would he sob & shrike?
And to be yong againe of Ioue beseke.

But and the cruell fates so fixed be
That time forepast can not retourne agayne,
This one request of Ioue yet prayed he:
That in such withered plight, and wretched paine,
As elde (accompanied with his lothsom trayne.)
Had brought on him, all were it woe and griefe.
He myght a while yet linger forth his lief,

And not so soone descend into the pit:
Where death, when he the mortall corps hath slayne,
With retcheles hande in grave doth couer it,
Thereafter neuer to enioye agayne
The gladsome light, but in the ground ylayne,
In depth of darkenes waste and weare to nought,
As he had neuer into the world been brought.

But who had seene him sobbing, howe he stoode
Vnto him selfe and howe he would bemone
His youth forepast, as though it wrought hym good
To talke of youth, al wer his youth foregone,
He would haue mused, & meruayld muche whereon
This wretched age should life desyre so fayne,
And knowes ful wel life doth but length his payne.

Crookebackt he was, toothshaken, and blere iyed,
Went on three feete, and sometime crept on fower,
With olde lame bones, that ratled by his syde,
His skalpe all pilde, & he with elde forlore:
His withered fist stil knocking at deathes dore,
Fumbling and drivueling as he drawes his breth,
For briefe the shape and messenger of death.

(295-336)

Here Sackville devotes six stanzas to Virgil's "tristisque Senectus." Sackville's Olde Age at times closely resembles the mysterious old man in Chaucer's *Pardoner's Tale*. "His witherd fist still knocking at dethe's dore" is surely an echo of

> And on the ground, which is my moodres gate.
> I knokke with my staf, bothe erly and late,
> And seye, "Leeve mooder, leet me in!"
> (729-31)

According to Kittredge, Chaucer's portrait is itself based on a Classical source, the first elegy of Maximianus.[8] Bacquet points to allusions to old age in other possible sources for Sackville's stanzas: Seneca's *Hercules Furens* and *Oedipus; The Castle of Perseveraunce* and *Everyman; The Pilgrimage of the Life of Man,* translated by Lydgate; Lydgate's *The Siege of Thebes* and *The Fall of Princes.*[9] The theme of old age is so common to the Middle Ages that wherever one turns a possible source lurks. Here Sackville's description is composed of elements from Classical antiquity and the English Middle Ages; some elements are more specifically attributable than others; the theme itself is a common one. Sackville, who joins and transforms the various elements, produced from a Medieval commonplace a portrait that is vivid, individual, sympathetic, and part of the fabric of his entire poem.

II *The* Complaint

Because the *Complaint* presents a tragical account of the Duke of Buckingham, the right hand of Richard III, Sackville, as might be expected, goes to contemporary chronicles for his main sources; but some Classical and Medieval borrowings are also found in this poem. Swart believes that the end of the *Complaint* is inspired by the *Aeniad,* that "it is a combination of the prophetic words at the end of the sixth book and the exclamation of Deiphobus," which he quotes.[10] This seems plausible, although the prophecy also contains echoes of Seneca. Virgil's lines on sleep and night (Book IV), translated by Surrey, follow.

> It was then night, the sounde and quiet slepe
> Had through the earth the weried bodyes caught.
> The woodes, the ragyng seas were falne to rest,
> When that the starres had halfe their course declined.
> The feldes whist, beastes, and fowles of divers hue,

And what so that in the brode lakes remainde,
Or yet among the bushy thickes of bryar,
Laide downe to slepe by silence of the night
Gan swage their cares, mindlesse of travels past.
(702-10)

Surrey's poetry seems to have had some effect on Sackville's beautiful description:

Mydnyght was cum, and every vitall thyng
With swete sound slepe theyr weary lyms dyd rest,
The beastes were still, the lytle byrdes that syng,
Nowe sweetely slept besides theyr mothers brest:
The olde and all were shrowded in theyr nest.
The waters calme, the cruel seas did ceas,
The wuds, the fyeldes, & all thinges held theyr peace.

The golden stars wer whyrlde amyd theyr race,
And on the earth did laugh wyth twinkling lyght,
When eche thing nestled in his restyng place,
Forgat dayes payne with pleasure of the nyght:
The Hare had not the greedy houndes in sight,
The fearfull Dear of death stoode not in doubt,
The Patrydge drept not of the Falcons foote.

The ougly Beare nowe mynded not the stake,
Nor how the cruell mastyues do hym tear,
The stag laye still vnroused from the brake,
The fomy boar feard not the hunters spear.
All thing was still in desert, bush and brear.
With quyet hart now from their trauailes rest,
Soundly they slept in midst of all their rest.
(547-67)

Valerius Maximus also provides Sackville with some material. Sackville wrote Maximus' name in the manuscript opposite the stanza beginning the story of Titus Clelius, and he goes to him for details not only in this story but also in the stories of Scipio and Milciades and Hannibal.[11] Plutarch provides the details for Sackville's account of Dionysius (267-87) and perhaps for part of the story of Darius (113-19).

Lydgate's *The Fall of Princes* is the work of the Middle Ages that Sackville most often goes to for his historical allusions. At times,

Sackville takes a detail or two; at other times, Sackville's wording is close to Lydgate's. The following account of Cyrus is Lydgate's:[12]

First this Cirus all pryncis dede excell
Bothe in conquest, victorie and bataile,
Off gold & tresour, as bookis off hym telle:
Kyngdamys to wynne he dede most preuaile;
And yit too vicis dede his herte assaile,
First couetise euere tencrece in good,
With a desir to sheede mennys blood.

. . . .

First she chargid to smyte off his hed,
When she thus hath the victorie off hym wonne.
And in a bath, that was off blood al red,
She gan it throwe, withynne a litle tonne.
And off despiht riht thus she hath begonne,
Most tirantli in his woful rage,
To dede Cirus to hauen this language:

"O thou Cirus, that whilom wer so wood
And so thrustleuh in thi tirannye,
Ageyne Nature to sheede manys blood,
So woluyssh was thyn hatful dropisie,
That merci non myhte it modefie,
Thyn etik ioyned, gredi and onstable,
With thrust off slauhtre ay to be vengable.
(Book II, 3767-73, 3879-92)

Below is Sackville's Cyrus:

Consyder Cyrus in your cruell thought,
A makeles prynce in ryches and in myght,
And weygh in minde the bloudy dedes he wrought,
In sheading which he set his whole delyght:
But see the guerdon lotted to this wyght,
He whose huge power no man might ouerthrowe,
Tomyris Queen with great despite hath slowe.

His head dismembred from his mangled corps,
Her selfe she cast into a vessell fraught
With clottered bloud of them that felt her force.
And with these wordes a iust reward she taught:
Drynke nowe thy fyll of thy desyred draught.

> Loe marke the fine that did this prynce befall:
> Marke not this one, but marke the ende of all.
> (85-98)

Sackville's main and direct source for the *Complaint* is Edward Hall's *Chronicle* (1548), but some details are found in Robert Fabyan's *Chronicle* (1516). Sir Thomas More's *The History of King Richard III* (1514) is the basis of all accounts of the reign of Richard III, including Hall's, so that More is the ultimate source of Sackville's narrative. Sackville, who reproduces the monstrous image of Richard III given in More, makes no attempt to present any shades of character because his primary interest is Buckingham, not Richard. Therefore, Richard emerges as a caricature of the King as Tyrant, while Buckingham appears as a more complex and tragic figure.

Most of the details of the story of Buckingham, his genealogy, his physical portrait, are found in Hall. Parallel passages abound. The following passage is from Hall:

> While this Busy searche was diligentely applied and put in execucion, Homfrey Banaster (were it more for feare of losse of lyfe and goodes, or attracted and prouoked by the auaricious desire of the thousand poundes) he bewrayed his gest and master to Ihon Mitton then shriefe of shropshire, whyche sodaynely with a stronge power of men in harnes apprehended the duke in a litle groue adioynynge to the mansion of Homfrey Banaster, and in greate hast and euyel spede conueighed him appareled in a pilled blacke cloke to the cytie of Salsburie where Kynge Richard then kepte his houshold.[13]

How much borrowing Sackville did is indicated by the parallel passage below:

> For by this wretche I beyng strayt betrayed,
> To one Iohn Mitton, shiriffe of Shropshire then,
> All sodaynely was taken, and conuayed
> To Salisbury, wyth rout of harnest men,
> Vnto kyng Rychard there encamped then:
> Fast by the citye with a myghtye hoste
> Withouten doome where head and lyfe I lost.
> (533-39)

Of course, Sackville deviates from Hall's account; his changes indicate that Sackville wishes to make Buckingham a sympathetic character. Although this point is discussed in Chapter 5, one example here will suggest how Sackville leaves his source for his purpose. Whereas Hall attributes the desertion of Buckingham's men to Buckingham's avarice and cruelty, Sackville emphasizes the fickleness of the mob:

> O let no prynce put trust in commontie,
> Nor hope in fayth of gyddy peoples mynde,
> But let all noble men take hede by me,
> That by the proofe to well the payne do fynde:
> Loe, where is truth or trust? or what could bynde
> The vayne people, but they will swarve and swaye,
> As chaunce bryngs chaunge, to dryve & draw that way?
> (421-27)

Sackville, therefore, wishing to soften his portrait of Buckingham, departs from his source in order to present a commonplace about the mob, one so familiar to readers of Shakespeare.

Three ballads now extant present some details on Buckingham and Banaster, the man who betrayed Buckingham.[14] For example, Sackville goes to the ballads which present three disasters befalling Banaster's children for his treachery rather than the four disasters presented by Hall. Here Sackville is aiming for greater credulity, which the ballads seem to provide.

In summary, then, for his *Complaint* Sackville goes primarily to Hall, gets some details from Fabyan and from some ballads, uses Lydgate for historical allusions, and goes to Virgil and Seneca for some trappings connected with tone. In both the *Complaint* and the "Induction" Sackville borrowed freely, but he was not servile to his sources. He elaborated, cut, joined, transformed, dramatized. His "plagiarism" was a characteristic of an age which affirmed the necessity of imitation. He preserved the Classical and Medieval traditions in his work, and his was a typically Renaissance synthesis.

CHAPTER 4

The "Induction"

IN the section "To the Reader" that precedes the "Induction," Baldwin tells his collaborators that Sackville's poetry is "so wel penned, that I woulde not have any verse thereof left out of our volume." He is the first in a long line of critics who have commented on the value of the poem. The most famous expression of praise is Saintsbury's, previously quoted, that Sackville's is the best poetry between Chaucer and Spenser. At the other extreme, C. S. Lewis discusses Sackville as a "drab verse" poet.[1] Other critics find their places between these estimates. Saintsbury is, however, much closer to a true evaluation of the "Induction" than Lewis, for the poem is a brilliant performance which can be compared with the best poems in the English language.

The "Induction," like the *Complaint,* is written in the rhyme royal stanza, seven lines of iambic pentameter rhyming *ababbcc.* Sackville chose the stanza associated with Chaucer and his followers; but, more important, he selected the stanza that is perfectly suited for serious verse and is especially effective in expressing sorrow and passion. The stanza is capable of great unity because the rhymes bind the stanza together and because the central couplet prepares us gradually for the final one. Sackville's metrical unit, the stanza, is usually also his grammatical unit, the sentence, so that his style can be described as taut.[2]

Rhyme, however, is not Sackville's strength, as Bacquet convincingly demonstrates. Sackville tends to repeat rhymes, to neglect them, or to present defective ones. Therefore, the stanza, although kept together in part by rhyme, is sometimes weakened by the choice of the rhyming words. This fault is one in the midst of many poetic excellences.

Like his contemporaries, Sackville was a slave to the syllable; and, at times, we can hear him count aloud to get his right accents.

But this mechanical effect is often subdued by the melody of his verse, especially the brilliant use of the long vowel to suggest "woe" — his favorite word — and the sighs of lamentation.

The Medieval tradition gives Sackville alliteration, which he uses relentlessly; approximately nine out of ten lines have some alliteration. Each of his alliterative lines is a well-knit unit, but the unity of the stanza is never sacrificed for the sake of the alliteration in one particular line, because the lines are connected by rhyming words. Since Sackville is careful to vary his long vowels, the alliteration is rarely burdensome. C. S. Lewis quotes three lines of Sackville and three lines from Sir Philip Sidney, and he praises Sidney's golden verse at the expense of Sackville's drab poetry. Lewis is especially negative about Sackville's alliteration in such lines as the following:

> O Sorrow, alas, sith Sorrow is thy name,
> And that to thee this drere doth well pertaine,
> In vayne it were to seeke to cease the same. . . .[3]

These lines, however, are not typical Sackville. They are "laborious," as Lewis states; but we must remark that this is the effect that Sackville wished to achieve in this part of the poem, where the heaviness of sorrow is emphasized.

In contrast to the lines just quoted, Sackville makes fine use of enjambement, which is closely tied to the thought of the poem, and which allows him to present an active narrative when he so desires.

We have noticed that Sackville is attached to the Middle Ages in his borrowings, in his stanza, and in his use of alliteration. He also uses archaisms, many directly from Chaucer. Most of these are specific words, but many are what we may regard as grammatical archaisms, like auxiliary verbs and infinitive forms.[4] These archaisms add to the charm of the poem and are suitable to the other-worldly quality of particular passages, but they never become so affected as to defeat Sackville's purpose. Sackville also loads his poem with nouns and adjectives, usually to effect his realistic portraitures and to give deliberate monotony to some of his verse. He is especially fond of longer nouns, which help make the poem more formal and serious, and which can often be used to enhance a line's musicality.

The "Induction" indicates that Sackville was thoroughly familiar with the principles of rhetoric, as Swart and Rubel amply demonstrate.[5] They find in Sackville's poem the figures of bar-

barism, epizeuxis, merismus, paroemion, prosonomasia, antonomasia, anadiplosis, traductio asyndeton, and so on. These difficult terms are useful only to the student skilled in sixteenth-century terminology, but I mention them to suggest the importance of Sackville's rhetorical training in the schools and to point to one source of Sackville's stylistic subtlety. To use simpler terms, Sackville uses to very good advantage repetition of a term in a single verse, contrast between terms in a single verse, hyperbole, and the simple comparison.

Commentary

In the narrative of the "Induction," it is winter; the chill of that cruel season has destroyed the bloom of summer; and Sackville is walking in the fields when night comes on suddenly. The change in the world about him, the death that winter brings to summer, makes him reflect on all the changes we find on earth, especially the fall of princes. He wishes that the fallen princes of England would describe their woes in order to warn those whom Fortune has left alive. At this thought, Sorrow, a figure clad in black and filled with woe, appears. She says that she has come from Hell to bemoan the destiny of those whom Fortune has placed in misery so that Sackville should realize that no earthly joy can endure, and she urges him to join her so that he can see and hear the plights of men overthrown by Fortune.

Sackville and Sorrow walk hand in hand through a thick wood, enter a deadly gulf, and arrive within the jaws of Hell. Here they encounter allegorical figures — Remorse of Conscience, Dread, Revenge, Misery, Greedy Care, Sleep, Old Age, Malady, Famine, Death, and War. On War's shield they find depicted the stories of illustrious men who have fallen; and the fall of Troy causes Sackville to lament. Sackville and Sorrow then continue their journey, sail over Acheron, pass by the barking, black Cerberus, and arrive in the great kingdoms of Hell — the home of the princes of renown who were once on the top of Fortune's wheel and are now thrust down. The first to come to them is Henry, Duke of Buckingham, who weepingly is about to utter his complaint. At this point the 553-line poem, the "Induction," ends.

This narrative outline, bare as it is, reveals that Sackville is interested in reflecting upon the important theme of mutability. The theme, an Elizabethan commonplace, is one which only an effective poet can make the reader feel. Sackville does so admirably, and "feel" is the proper word to indicate Sackville's achievement. Although Sackville is a didactic poet in a didactic collection, the "Induction," contrary to most critical opinions of the poem, is more a mood piece than a didactic pronouncement on mutability. Sackville states that the fall of princes can serve as a lesson to those princes alive — the "mirrour" forever reflecting — but he expends his poetic energy on description, not on moral reflection; on mood and atmosphere, not on thoughtful meditation. The reflection and meditation are present; indeed, the descriptions obviously influence our thoughts on the changes in life. But the theme of mutability is felt more than it is pondered; it affects us first emotionally, then intellectually.

Sackville is conventional in setting his poem in the out-of-doors and in describing the natural world before his guide comes to lead him to the underworld; but, instead of choosing the spring for his background — the usual season for Medieval poets who stress the singing of birds, the freshness of the air, the joy of the spirit — Sackville chooses winter, which allows him to evoke immediately a dark tragic world:

The Wrathfull winter prochinge on a pace,
With blustring blastes had al ybared the treen,
And olde Saturnus with his frosty face
With chilling colde had pearst the tender green:
The mantels rent, wherein enwrapped been
The gladsom groves that nowe laye ouerthrowen,
The tapets torne, and euery blome downe blowen.

The soyle that earst so seemely was to seen
Was all despoyled of her beauties hewe:
And soot freshe flowers (wherwith the sommers queen
Had clad the earth) now Boreas blastes downe blewe.
And small fowles flocking, in theyr sond did rewe
The winters wrath, wherwith eche thing defaste
In woful wise bewayld the sommer past.

Hawthorne had lost his motley lyverye,
The naked twigges were shivering all for colde:
And dropping downe the teares abundantly,
Eche thing (me thought) with weping eye me tolde
The cruell season, bidding me withholde
My selfe within, for I was gotten out
Into the fieldes where as I walkte about.
(1-21)

Winter to Sackville the poet becomes more than a mere setting; it is a force that wrathfully devastates the natural world and destroys the summer in things. Sackville allows us to feel, if only fleetingly, what *was* — the trees were once filled with foliage, the green was tender, the groves were "gladsome," the flowers bloomed. The birds once sang a happier song; now they complain of winter's tyranny. This setting is the very landscape of tragedy, and the comparison of what was and is becomes the foundation of a contemplation of fallen princes, of tragic heroes. Winter is presented as an inevitable force, as inevitable as mutability.

By giving to aspects of the natural world human feelings, a romantic device, Sackville is able to suggest the alliance between external nature and the emotions of the speaker, the "I" of the poem. Winter is wrathful, each thing destroyed bewails its fate, the twigs shiver and cry. The transition to the "I" who has observed these wintry happenings becomes easy. And the sounds of woe — the long vowels work very effectively here — fill the air and the speaker's heart. He becomes tenderly one with the natural victims of an inevitable force, and his observations trigger his thoughts on "the sundry changes that in earth we fynde."

The "I" of line 20 is strongly felt throughout the poem, for the narrator responds emotionally to the figures he meets and to the changing world around him. His responses do not cover the wide emotional range we find in the responses of Dante's pilgrim, but the "I" — the narrator or the poet — sighs, moans, and weeps; he feels great fear and great pity. We find no scorn or resentment in him, no vindictiveness, no touch of humor. His own temperament helps to inform the gloom of the poem, for nothing relieves us from the misery and despair.

The coming of night brings forth four stanzas that present specific astronomical details, again a conventional concern in medieval poems; but the description seems too specific, too academic. We find the usual "azure skyes," "bluddy Mars," "pale Cinthea," but we have been so slowed up by these conventional allusions that the poet's assertion at the end of these stanzas — "The darke had dimmed the daye ear I was ware" — seems hard to believe.

The winter and the night, the physical setting, produce an emotional atmosphere and call forth a general reflection:

> And sorowing I to see the sommer flowers,
> The liuely greene, the lusty leas forlorne,

> The sturdy trees so shattered with the showers,
> The fieldes so fade that floorisht so beforne,
> It taught me wel all earthly thinges be borne
> To dye the death, for nought long time may last.
> The sommers beauty yeeldes to winters blast.
> (50-56)

This contemplation of mortality stems gracefully from the previous description, and the last line of the stanza summarizes what we have already heard in greater detail. The poet looks up to the stars, thick in the night's sky, and suddenly thinks of the changes we find on earth. The reference to the stars is perfectly placed here, for the stars are related in the Elizabethan mind to the notion of Fortune: it was generally believed that the stars dictated the mutability of earthly things.[6] A look at the stars, therefore, would call to mind the fortunes of men; and the physical once again leads to the philosophical.

The poet's musing on general mutability takes on a specific cast when he thinks of the fall of princes — the central focus of the tragical narratives found in *The Mirror for Magistrates.* When he wishes that the princes describe their woes "To warne the rest whom fortune left alive," Sackville's didactic intent is openly stated, the mirror will be set up, and the one who will make his wish come true appears.

The personification Sorrow comes to the poet suddenly, but she is very much a part of the setting:

> Her body small forwithered and forespent,
> As is the stalke that sommers drought opprest.

She, like the natural world, has been devastated. Old, withered, and spent, Sorrow is given the appropriate actions and gestures for what she represents — she sighs, cries, shrieks, wrings her hands, tears her hair. Indeed, she is "a piteous wight," whose dreadful condition causes the poet to stand aghast between "dread and dolour." Both fear and pity seize him, but his doleful voice does manage to utter: "Tell what thou art, and whence." She identifies herself as a creature endlessly tormented among the furies in Hell:

> Whence come I am, the drery destinie
> And luckeles lot for to bemone of those,
> Whom Fortune in this maze of miserie
> Of wretched chaunce most wofull myrrours chose

That when thou seest how lightly they did lose
Theyr pompe, theyr power, & that they thought most sure,
Thou mayest soone deeme no earthly ioye may dure.
(113-19)

Sackville has Sorrow sound again the mutability theme, specifically mentioning Fortune and mirrors and the pomp and power of princes.

Sorrow is emblematic, but not static; for she proceeds to fall down, to dash herself against the ground, and to shriek. The poet's limbs go cold, but his spirits revive enough for him to tell her that he, himself a man of sorrow, wishes to comfort her in pain. Sorrow's emotions at hearing this statement reach hyperbolic proportions:

I had no sooner spoken of a syke
But that the storme so rumbled in her brest,
As Eolus could neuer roare the like,
And showers downe rayned from her iyen so fast,
That all bedreynt the place, till at the last
Well eased they the dolour of her minde,
As rage of rayne doth swage the stormy wynde.
(141-47)

And with a fearful urgency she verbally pulls the poet along with her on a journey to Hell:

Cum, cum, (quod she) and see what I shall shewe,
Cum heare the playning, and the bytter bale
Of worthy men, by Fortune ouerthrowe.
Cum thou and see them rewing al in rowe.
They were but shades that erst in minde thou rolde.
Cum, cum with me, thine iyes shall them beholde.
(149-54)

The repetitions ravish, and the poet is ready to follow the woeful guide, but not before he is surprised that she is able to read his mind, thereby making him recognize her as a Goddess who has come to him in earthly shape "to wayle and rue this worldes uncertayne." A guide is necessary for the journey to the underworld — Virgil had the Sybil; Dante, Virgil; Sackville, Sorrow. The journeys taken by Virgil, Dante, and Sackville are very different; but the journey itself is archetypal.

The journey to the underworld is a deep-seated, general form for ordering experience; and, therefore, it was widely used by poets. It also contains within it a density of suggestion which affects anyone reading of such a journey. The source of the potency of the journey motif cannot be fully explained by external statement, whether it be historical, philosophical, religious, or psychological. Suffice to say that the journey to the end fulfills our human wishes and fills us with a sense of mystery and, at times, horror. Sackville's journey stresses the horror, and for this reason Sackville's genius is considered to be more Dantesque than Virgilian.[7] Sackville, like Homer and Virgil and Dante before him, uses the great metaphor of the world of the dead; but, of the four poets, only Dante and Sackville reveal the real terror of the visit, and Sackville does not even share Dante's doctrinal purpose of displaying rewards and punishments. One of Sackville's dead tells his own story, and Sackville's allegorical representations bewail their misery; but religious doctrine plays no part in the presentation. The allegorical figures represent qualities, but they carry little symbolism and they lack the multiplicity of dimension we associate with Dante's figures. Sackville's representations are not symbols, but images; and Sackville stresses the sensuous, the external, the physical, the concrete, rather than the allegorical and doctrinal.

Sackville's more limited purpose is clearly evident when we consider the "wood" to which the poet and Sorrow come. In Dante, the wood is a place of moral bewilderment; and its interpretation on both an allegorical and a doctrinal level is important for a proper understanding of Dante's poem. In Sackville, the wood is merely the starting place for a journey. It acquires no weight of allegory; the thickness of the wood that Sackville alludes to is the literal one of density.

As Sorrow leads the poet — "hand in hand" — through the thick, they hear sounds of dogs so terrifying that the poet falls on the ground "halfe distraught" and desires not to visit Hell. But his guide removes his dread, and they come to "the place" — a word repeated four times and one effectively suspenseful in its vagueness. Sackville presents a vivid description of Lake Averne — his direct source is Virgil, as Chapter 3 demonstrated — and uses sound and physical detail to stress the horror of the place. Rubbish grows in the gulf, "with fowle blacke swelth in thickned lumpes that lyes,/ Which up in the ayer such stinking vapors throwes/ That over there, may flye no fowle but dyes,/ Choakt with the pestilent savours that aryse." The lines read as thickly as the lumps, and the bird reference is especially effective, for the creature of the air, the heavens, and freedom can find only death in the fumy atmosphere of Hell.

The allegorical personifications appear, one at a time, in succession. The regularity of the succession of misery — like, incidentally, the regularity of the succession of tragical narratives in *The Mirror for Magistrates* — makes the misery seem as inevitable as mutability. The vignettes of woe take up almost two hundred lines of the poem. The personifications are described with great force of expression and with obvious care for the concrete detail. Sackville allows the physical details to indicate the anguish and passions of those he meets at Hell's jaws. For the most part, the physiognomy is used to reflect emotion and to signify what the figure represents. One of the two stanzas on Remorse of Conscience, the first of the procession, concentrates on her eyes:

> Her iyes vnstedfast rolling here and there,
> Whurld on eche place, as place that vengeaunce brought,
> So was her minde continually in feare,
> Tossed and tormented with the tedious thought
> Of those detested crymes which she had wrought:
> With dreadful cheare and lookes throwen to the skye,
> Wyshyng for death, and yet she could not dye.
> (225-31)

The eyes, madly whirling and rolling, effectively indicate a mind disturbed to the point of wishing for death. Conscience is at work, and the eyes allow us to see all.

The hair on Dread's head is standing up, and Revenge is gnashing her teeth. (The stanza on Revenge spits with the "f" sound — "But frets within so farforth with the fyer/ Of wreaking flames . . . . ") Miserie — called Povertie in the Hearsey edition — appears with a lean face and "handes consumed to the bone." Greedy Care (Hearsey's Busie Labour) has flesh "deepe dented in," Maladie has no color on her face, and Famine has a "gaping mouth." War has a "visage grym" and "sterne lookes." Olde Age, as we would expect, has a "beard al hoare, his iyes hollow and blynde."

These facial details, concrete and apparent, reflect the condition of the personifications; but so do actions and gestures. Dread, filled with fear, "searcht every place" with "a gastly looke." Miserie feeds on whatever crumbs come to him. Greedy Care is always "brushing up the breres," bruising his knuckles, and working day and night. Slepe is "flat on the ground," Maladie is sick in bed, Olde Age is "poring on the ground" and forever "knocking at deathes dore." Famine gnashes her own bones and snatches at whatever she sees with her "tearyng nayles." Death shakes his dart, and War carries his bloody sword and shield. These actions and gestures, although lacking refined discrimination of tone, are accurate enough to have a convincing emblematic relationship to the facts of life.

Some of these descriptive stanzas belong with the best in our language. The following stanza on Slepe, — a popular Elizabethan theme receiving beautiful treatment by Sidney (*Astrophel and Stella,* Sonnet 39), Daniel (*Delia,* Sonnet 49), and Shakespeare *(2 Henry IV)* — surely deserves the praise it has received:

> The bodyes rest, the quyete of the hart,
> The travayles ease, the still nightes feer was he.
> And of our life in earth the better parte,
> Reuer of sight, and yet in whom we see
> Thinges oft that tide, and ofte that neuer bee.
> Without respect esteming equally
> Kyng Cresus pompe, and Irus pouertie.
> (288-94)

The stanzas on Olde Age present a sensitive picture of that human condition. Not only is the physical description effective and haunting, but the figure's futile longing to be young again strikes a human chord that is both pathetic and truthful:

> But and the cruell fates so fixed be
> That time forepast can not retourne agayne,
> This one request of Ioue yet prayed he:
> That in such withered plight, and wretched paine,
> As elde (accompanied with his lothsom trayne.)
> Had brought on him, all were it woe and griefe.
> He myght a while yet linger forth his lief,
>
> And not so soone descend into the pit:
> Where death, when he the mortall corps hath slayne,
> With retcheles hande in grave doth couer it,
> Thereafter neuer to enioye agayne
> The gladsome light, but in the ground ylayne,
> In depth of darkenes waste and weare to nought,
> As he had neuer into the world been brought.
> (309-22)

Much of the effectiveness of these descriptive stanzas on the allegorical figures stems from Sackville's use of parallels and contrasts. He produces echoes of the opening description of winter's desolation, which tend to bind the poem and to suggest the unrelenting quality of the world's woe. Miserie, for example, has little protection against "the winters blast" and must make his bed "the hard colde grounde." Olde Age is withered and hoary, his summery youth is in a "time forepast," never to return again. Death is "heavy and colde"; it is vain to fight against his force, which is inevitable, like winter's.

Some parallels help to bind the specific portraits together. The nakedness of Death — the skeleton in his usual dance — is followed by a description of Warre's naked sword. The unsteady and tormented eyes of Remorse of Conscience is followed by the searching fearful eyes of Dread. Revenge gnashes her teeth for ire, Famine gnashes her teeth for hunger. Miserie, with staff in hand, braves the winter; Olde Age knocks with his staff at death's door in the winter of his life. The dart of Death is followed by the sword of Warre.

Sackville often juxtaposes elements in his description, but not for purposes of expansion — the usual result of juxtaposition in Gothic art; he uses the device for concentration since the dominant tone always remains despair. The frenzied activity of Greedy Care is followed by the restful stanzas on Sleep. (In the Hearsey edition, the rest of Sleep is followed by the menacing gestures of War.) Maladie, who has food but cannot eat it, is followed by Famine, who could eat but has no food. Death — "His bodie dight with nought but bones" — precedes War "in glitteryng armes yclad."

The reactions of the narrator also help to support the dominant tone and to unite the vignettes. His sympathy and terror is felt throughout. Revenge causes his limbs to tremble; he looks on Miserie's condition "with tender ruth"; he cannot refrain from tears when he sees Famine's desperation. Death's dart frightens him most — a good touch, for he, being mortal, must eventually take a second unreturnable trip to the underworld.

In short, the stock allegorical figures are animated by Sackville's vivid concreteness and sustained energy. The portraits are held together by comparison and contrast. The narrator's reactions give the stanzas an added dimension of pathos and terror. And this section of the poem is dense with sounds of woe and rhythmically insists on the wretched condition of man. All of these elements of

Sackville's art bear witness to the power of Sackville's creative imagination in working with sources discussed in Chapter 3.

Painted on the shield of Warre are scenes of battle and bloodshed involving famous men of history. These illustrations take up eleven stanzas of the "Induction," a section bathed in blood. The pace of the poem takes on speed in presenting the slaughters, but the density of the atmosphere remains. The feeling of constriction that we feel at the jaws of Hell as we see and hear the wailing abstractions remains a feeling of constriction — but this time it is caused by the confinement of a shield and by the thickness of blood.

Sackville rushes through the illustrious examples, disposing of Darius, Alexander, Hannibal, Scipio, Pompey, Caesar, Scilla, Marius, Cyrus, Xerxes, and the city Thebes in thirty lines. This section of the poem is not so much a narrative as a quick listing, for Sackville seems more interested in the fact of slaughter than in the description of it, although the blood flows freely. He displays the Medieval and Elizabethan fondness for classical allusions, but he does little to transform the bookish quality of a listing. (How different is his treatment of allusions in the *Complaint*.) When Sackville comes to the depiction of the fall of Troy, however, he dwells on it for six stanzas. In this section, he presents detailed narration; the poet reacts to the illustration, as he did to the woeful personifications. In this section he says that, by observing the fall of Troy, "we learne" that nothing prevails — thereby forcefully sounding the mutability theme.

The details of Troy's fall are vividly presented in this speedy narration:

> The flames vpspring, and cruelly they crepe
> From wall to roofe, til all to cindres waste,
> Some fyer the houses where the wretches slepe,
> Sum rushe in here, sum run in there as fast.
> In euery where or sworde or fyer they taste.
> The walles are torne, the towers whurld to the ground,
> There is no mischiefe but may there be found.
> (456-62)

The repetitions rush us along — "some" . . . "sum" . . . "sum." Cassandra is hauled from "Pallas house" and hemmed in by the Greeks; Priam seeks in vain for arms, is killed by Pyrrhus, and is bathed in blood; the ashes of Ilium are burning red. The narrator must weep and wail: "Troy alas" . . . "O Troy, Troy . . . ." The lament and description bear a didactic burden — for the fall of Troy was to the Renaissance mind the epitome of tragedy, the example *par excellence* of the workings of Time and Change, the ancient proof that great cities, like great men, must fall:

> . . . cities, towres, wealth, world, and al shall quayle.
> No manhoode, might, nor nothing mought preuayle,
> Al were there prest ful many a prynce and piere
> And many a knight that solde his death full deere.
> (445-48)

Troy assumes added importance in this poem, for it is the last illustration on Warre's shield to be described, and it also marks the end of the narrator's "stay" at the jaws of Hell. It fittingly concludes a succession of descriptive vignettes that depict misery, it sustains the melancholy mood, and it illuminates the theme of mutability — a theme we sometimes lose sight of when concentrating on the brilliant descriptions of the woeful personifications.

As Sorrow and the poet continue on their journey, we see Acheron, "a lothsome lake to tell/ That boyles and bubs up swelth as blacke as hell"; and across it Charon ferries ghosts. The visitors, linked "hand in hand," are placed in a boat that brings them to the bank where Cerberus barks. The phrase "hand in hand" connects the beginning of the journey to the journey's end, for the same words were used when Sorrow led the poet through the thick wood. The necessity for linking hands not only indicates the physical difficulty of the journey and the fright that the poet feels; it also physically and temperamentally joins the sorrowful poet to the poetical abstraction Sorrow. Their closeness can never be forgotten.

The deep darkness of the cave where Cerberus, "the hydeous hound of hell," dwells, added to the blackness of the boiling Lake Acheron, strongly returns us to the image at the beginning of the journey of that other lake, Averne, where all was "as blacke as pitche." And the horror of the hell that they now come to, with its emphasis on the sounds of despair, recalls all the woe we have encountered up to this point. With stately majesty the following stanzas brilliantly evoke the terror of Hell:

> Thence cum we to the horrour and the hel,
> The large great kyngdomes, and the dreadful raygne
> Of Pluto in his trone where he dyd dwell,
> The wyde waste places, and the hugye playne:

> The waylinges, shrykes, and sundry sortes of payne,
> The syghes, the sobbes, the diepe and deadly groane,
> Earth, ayer, and all resounding playnt and moane.
>
> Here pewled the babes, and here the maydes vnwed
> with folded handes theyr sory chaunce bewayled,
> Here wept the gyltles slayne, and louers dead,
> That slewe them selues when nothyng els auayled;
> A thousand sortes of sorrowes here that wayled
> with sighes and teares, sobs, shrykes, and all yfere,
> That (oh alas) it was a hel to heare.
> (505-18)

The previous "cums" of Sorrow, looking forward, have now led to the present "cum" of our dark destination. The different sounds — each of a different quality — are one in indicating the black despair. The specific references to babes, maids unwed, the guiltless, and lovers suggest that no one escapes the ultimate darkness. (The unwed maids are pictured with "folded hands," a quiet and sorrowful pose; and the portrayal contrasts to the hectic hands that tore flesh and pulled hair, and to the "hand in hand" of Sorrow and the poet.) The "oh alas" of the narrator seems to spring from his very depths, and it reinforces his other similar reactions to the anguish and terror around him. "A hel to heare" highlights the devastating quality of the sounds in Hell. The cadence of the verse in these stanzas is rich and stately, the descriptions apt, and all that came before seems to reverberate here.

Sackville gives us no relief, for even now the poet is weeping, and Sorrow is lamenting, "heaving to the skyes/ Her wretched handes." Sorrow speaks to the poet:

> Loe here (quoth Sorowe) Prynces of renowne,
> That whilom sat on top of Fortunes wheele
> Nowe layed ful lowe, like wretches shurled downe,
> Euen with one frowne, that stayed but with a smyle,
> And nowe behold the thing that thou erewhile,
> Saw only in thought, and what thou now shalt heare
> Recompt the same to Kesar, King, and Pier.
> (526-32)

The travelers have reached their destination, and Sorrow will now actualize what Sackville was thinking about in the poem's beginning. We are back to the notion of the fall of princes and Fortune's wheel. The first fallen prince appears, and his description, presented in concrete physical detail, make him one with Sorrow and similar to Remorse of Conscience.

> Then first came Henry duke of Buckingham,
> His cloke of blacke al pilde and quite forworne,
> Wringing his handes, and Fortune ofte doth blame,
> Which of a duke hath made him nowe her skorne.
> With gastly lookes as one in maner lorne,
> Oft spred his armes, stretcht handes he ioynes as fast,
> With ruful chere, and vapored eyes vpcast.
>
> His cloke he rent, his manly breast he beat,
> His heare al torne about the place it laye,
> My hart so molte to see his griefe so great,
> As felingly me thought it dropt awaye:
> His iyes they whurled about withouten staye,
> With stormy syghes the place dyd so complayne,
> As if his hart at eche had burst in twayne.
> (533-46)

We note the black clothing, the ghastly looks, the hands — wringing, and then stretched and joined — the tearing of the hair, the ripping of the clothes, whirling eyes, and stormy sighs. Once again the physical and psychological come together, as in the description of the allegorical figures; and Buckingham becomes a logical and esthetic extension of all that came before — and the unity is reinforced by the poet's reaction to him as to the others.

Buckingham's actions and gestures, as emblematic as those of the abstractions, become humanized when he finds it difficult to speak. The "sighes" that choke him seem real indeed: he has difficulty beginning his "doleful tale," but he finally recovers his voice, swallows his own tears, and begins his complaint against Fortune — "On cruel Fortune weping thus he playnde." The complaint itself is Sackville's second poem, a logical extension of the "Induction."

The "Induction," a great independent poem, stands alone in both intent and accomplishment in an influential collection of tragical narratives. It is, as the title indicates, the beginning of a collection, as Sackville conceived it; but the larger purpose was not accomplished, and so it stands as the introduction to only one narrative and has obvious connections with that narrative. Sackville forcefully sounds the theme of Fortune and Mutability in the

Complaint, the very theme that the poet thinks about in the beginning of the "Induction." But the "Induction," although didactic in places, is essentially a mood piece that is brilliant in its evocation of atmosphere, vivid in its imagery, concrete in its description, effective in its fusion of sense and sound, and unified in concept and performance.

CHAPTER 5

The Complaint

THE *Complaint of Henry, Duke of Buckingham* has not received so favorable a critical reception as the "Induction." Critics invariably compare the two poems, and praise the "Induction" at the expense of the *Complaint*. The *Complaint* is either considered "dull on the whole,"[1] or applauded for parts which usually are contrasted to the rest of the poem.[2] To compare the two poems is a necessary exercise, not for the sake of giving each a rating, a pointless task, but to demonstrate the essential differences in Sackville's intention and execution. Marguerite Hearsey believes that the two poems are one because they were printed together in a single manuscript, and her suggestion has been followed by most commentators. But their physical togetherness in a manuscript and their many similarities should not obscure the fact that we are dealing with two different poems, each affecting the reader in a different way.

The figure of Henry, Duke of Buckingham, obviously links the two poems; for, as he ends the "Induction," he is ready to utter his complaint; and the *Complaint* is this utterance. The complaint monologue itself is a genre with its own history, for it is a common Medieval poetic form found in the *chanson de geste*. It appears in Latin as the *planctus* and in Anglo-Saxon literature as the lament, and it can be traced back to the Old Testament. As a monologue, it differs from the "Induction," which contains dialogue and which presents an interplay of characters. As a complaint, however, it continues the atmosphere of grief of the "Induction," and it moans the sounds of woe, this time coming from the man presenting the lament.

Buckingham seems at times very similar to the personifications we meet in the "Induction." He has the restless thoughts of Remorse of Conscience who was "Tossed and tormented with the tedious thought/ Of those detested crymes which she had wrought." Buckingham is also tormented: "With restles thought so is the guylty minde/ Turmoyled, and never feeleth ease or stay." He has the fear of Dread, for his heavy burden of guilt makes him act "Much like the felon that pursued by nights,/ Starts at eche bushe as his foe were in sight." He typifies Revenge in his curses against Banaster, the man who betrays him to Richard III. And Buckingham throughout the *Complaint* displays the many characteristics of Sorrow — the pale complexion, swollen eyes, sighs of every quality, tears that run like rivers, and the wringing and flinging of hands, the woe. In short, Buckingham, the one lamenter in the *Complaint,* is a composite of many of the emblematic characters of the "Induction." This portrayal permits him to be more than a stereotype; for in not representing one quality, as does each abstraction, he seems more human, more real — even, shall we say, more historical.

The personifications in the "Induction" are echoed also in the descriptions of Richard III and in some of the historical illustrations. Dread, for example, appears again in the stanzas depicting the fear of tyrants. Phereus, who can trust no one, not even his wife, causes his slaves to walk before him, and "whorling in his head/ His rolling iyen, he searcheth here and there/ The diepe daunger that he so sore did feare." Like the "Induction," the *Complaint* contains illustrations from history, exempla which help Sackville illuminate a point he wishes to make. However, these illustrations consume much more space in the *Complaint* — about one-quarter of the lines in the *Complaint* as opposed to one-seventh in the "Induction." Some of these are quick references to historic figures; others are realistic glimpses of the past that have intrinsic interest, and two effective examples are the violent death of Cyrus and the agony of Alexander at the death of Clitus. These exempla tend to slow the narrative, but their number indicates that Sackville is more interested in the lessons that history teaches than in the pace of his narrative.

This last observation points to what is the most important difference between the two poems: the *Induction* states the didactic intent and presents what is essentially a descriptive mood piece; but the *Complaint* states its didactic intent again and again, and never forgets it. For this reason, the second poem contains more maxims, more lesson-teaching aphorisms, more exempla, and has less description, less color, less variety. The mirror in the *Complaint* is always reflecting, not primarily in order to please the senses or to disturb the emotions, but to affect the mind, to teach.

Another important difference is that the poet-narrator does not react to Buckingham's plight so often as he does to Sorrow and the figures he meets at Hell's gate in the "Induction." This difference stems from the monologue form, since the reactions of Buckingham, who is relating his misfortune, are of greater importance than the reactions of the listener to him. The poet-narrator in the *Complaint* is essentially a listener, but in the "Induction" he is the center of attention — the wanderer, observer, and talker. The reader of the *Complaint* is also a listener; and, although we identify with the speaker Buckingham, our emotions are not triggered by the reactions of the poet. For the most part, Buckingham's plight has to affect us directly or not at all.

The *Complaint,* which uses the rhyme-royal stanza, as does the "Induction," displays most of the characteristics of verse and language found in that poem. It contains greater stiffness in the language, more explicit statements, and less color in the descriptions. We find fewer archaisms in the *Complaint,* which once again indicates that Sackville is more interested in message than in the flavor of his presentation. In general, then, threads of similarity — in verse and language, in exempla, in echoes of the allegorical abstractions, and in the atmosphere of grief — bind the two poems and cause us to think of the "Induction" when we read the *Complaint.* But these threads do not make the two poems one, because they are not strong enough to contain two different forms and two different intents. The *Complaint* is more intellectual than emotional, more didactic than descriptive; therefore, it is a less colorful and less immediate poem than the "Induction." But it is perfectly suited to its author's intent, and has its own dimension of worth.

Commentary

In *The Complaint of Henry, Duke of Buckingham,* a 777-line complaint monologue, Buckingham tells how he aided Richard III in his rise to the crown, how he rebelled against Richard, and how he was betrayed by his friend Banaster and was led to his death. This historical narrative account, based primarily on Hall's *Chronicle,* also contains sections on Revenge, Conscience, the dread of tyrants, and the falsity of mobs, all supported by historical exempla. The monologue is presented, as Buckingham and Sackville remind us often, to teach a lesson to posterity.

The poem's opening stanzas immediately stress the notion of Fortune and indicate Sackville's intention:

> Who trustes to much in honours highest trone
> And warely watche not slye dame Fortunes snare:
> Or who in courte will beare the swaye alone,
> And wysely weygh not howe to wyeld the care,
> Beholde he me, and by my death beware:
> Whom flattering Fortune falsely so begilde
> That loe she slewe, where earst ful smooth she smylde.
>
> And Sackeuylle sith in purpose nowe thou hast
> The woful fal of prynces to discryve,
> Whom Fortune both vplyft, and gayn downe cast,
> To shewe thereby the vnsuerty in this life,
> Marke wel my fal, which I shal shewe belive.
> And paynt it furth that All estates may knowe:
> Haue they the warning, and be mine the woe.
> (1-14)

Here and throughout the poem Fortune is the conventional Medieval goddess — false, flattering, smiling, sly, beguiling, capricious, she lifts up and casts down. This up-down movement typifies Buckingham's career and the careers of all protagonists of tragical narratives.

"Behold he me, and by my death beware" forcefully presents Buckingham's purpose in telling his tale; for he will be the mirror — "behold" — with which Sackville, who is named directly, can "shewe" the "unsuerty in this life." Such words as "marke wel my fal" and "warning" accentuate Sackville's didactic intent and place the *Complaint* solidly in the mirror tradition, thereby making it one among many tragical narratives which will serve as a "mirror for magistrates."

Having expressed his purpose in presenting his lament, and having indicated the qualities of Fortune, Buckingham then presents his own ancestry, emphasizing that he was fortunate in his birth and noble blood and that he was endowed by God with gifts. Immediately, however, Buckingham asks a question that touches a crucial aspect of man's life: "But what avayles his (God's) gifts where fayles his grace?" This question is the first of many asked in the poem, all of which point to the uncertainties in life and to the mystery of existence. The mood of the poem comes very close, therefore, to being interrogative.

Although Buckingham was born with the advantages to make him "a prince withouten peer," God's grace seemed to be withheld and Fortune was at work to bring him low. His ancestors fought faithfully for their masters, but they died in battle — "But what may boot to stay the sisters three?" This reference to destiny, this question about the mystery of Fate, which closely follows references to God's grace and the notion of Fortune, again pinpoints Sackville's philosophical concern. Within the first forty lines of his poem, Sackville causes his lamenter to mention and ask questions about the plight of man in this uncertain world and the forces that bring him down.

How appropriate that Sackville follows Buckingham's stanza on the working of the three sisters and the death of his grandfather with these words:

> In place of whom, as it befel my lot,
> Like on a stage, so stept I in strayt waye,
> Enjoying there but wofully god wot,
> As he that had a slender part to playe:
> To teache therby, in earth no state may stay,
> But as our partes abridge or length our age
> So passe we all while others fyll the stage.
> (43-49)

The stage image is an Elizabethan commonplace, one well known because of Shakespeare's frequent use of it in his plays; but, by placing it here, Sackville gives the image an uncommon force. Coming after the notions of up-and-down, Fortune, and God's grace and destiny, it brilliantly accentuates the changes in life — "in earth no state may stay" — which is the poem's theme; it stresses the fleeting quality of life; and it suggests that the stage will always be filled with players who will experience the changes, thus speaking directly to the very readers and magistrates who are now on the stage and who could, perhaps, learn from Buckingham's experience. The stage image intensifies and sharpens the poignancy of man's "stay" in this world, and pinpoints the dramatic quality of a historical character's lament.

The poem's stage is now set for the introduction of Richard III, who was to the Elizabethans the King as Tyrant. The characterization, or caricature, of Richard as solidified in More's *Life* and as transmitted through Hall was, as we have noted, the basis for

Sackville's depiction. Buckingham talks of his alliance with Richard:

> For when the fates had reft that royal prince
> Edward the fowrth, chiefe myrrour of that name,
> The duke and I fast ioyned ever since,
> In faythfull love, our secrete driftes to frame:
> What he thought best, to me so seemde the same,
> My selfe not bent so much for to aspyer,
> As to fulfyl that greedy dukes desyre.
> (57-63)

Although Buckingham is indicating that he was not so ambitious for himself as he was for Richard, the word "love" — a rare one in the *Complaint* — emotionally binds Buckingham to Richard and makes them both responsible for Richard's sins. The greed may be Richard's, but his desires are fulfilled with Buckingham's help. The Duke mentions Richard's "restles minde sore thyrsting after rule" and repeats the notion of "eygre thirst" in the next stanza. Richard's drive for power, the fact that "he ran so headlong swyft," points ahead to Shakespeare's emphasis in *Richard III* on Richard's energy and ability to go on without stopping for breath. Eventually, Buckingham will stop being Richard's helper, will run out of breath, but for now he helps Richard kill his way to the top:

> And I most cursed caytief that I was,
> Seeing the state vnstedfast howe it stood,
> His chief complyce to bryng the same to passe,
> Vnhappy wretche consented to theyr blood.
> (78-81)

Having directly expressed his guilt, he presents, what is characteristic for the Buckingham of the *Complaint,* overt moralizing:

> Ye Kinges and Piers that swim in worldly good,
> In seekyng blud the ende aduert you playne,
> And see if bloud ey aske not blud agayne.
> (82-84)

That "blud will have blood" is one of the most important ideas in the poem and helps to unify it, for Buckingham later presents his own demand for vengeance. Here Buckingham utters the maxim and presents a series of historical illustrations that depict the savage deaths of leaders who are killed because of their own cruelty: Cyrus, Cambises, Brutus and Cassius, Bessus, and Alexander. The vivid stanzas on Cyrus effectively indicate Sackville's preoccupation with blood:

> Consyder Cyrus in your cruell thought,
> A makeles prynce in ryches and in myght,
> And weygh in minde the bloudy dedes he wrought,
> In sheading which he set his whole delyght:
> But see the guerdon lotted to this wyght,
> He whose huge power no man might ouerthrowe,
> Tomyris Queen with great despite hath slowe.
>
> His head dismembred from his mangled corps,
> Her selfe she cast into a vessell fraught
> With clottered bloud of them that felt her force.
> And with these wordes a iust reward she taught:
> Drynke nowe thy fyll of thy desyred draught.
> Loe marke the fine that did this prynce befall:
> Marke not this one, but marke the ende of all.
> (85-98)

These two stanzas not only reveal the horror of the death but also emphasize "the just reward," how blood leads to blood. The stanzas also contain Sackville's constant reminder that we must learn from this example — "marke . . . marke . . . marke." The phrase "Drynke now thy fyll" allows us to remember Richard's thirst and his eventual end. In short, these are most effective stanzas because the vivid description and the poet's didactic intent are successfully fused.

The account of Cambises' death ends with the line: "So just is God in al his dreadfull doomes." Brutus and Cassius "justly" fell, Bessus' was a "just deserved fall," and Alexander's death was "just rewarde." In all of these illustrations, therefore, blood leads to blood, and the cruel deaths are just and deserved — with God's judgment operating. The Revenge theme, so important to Elizabethan drama, seems to have significant beginnings not only in the Senecan dramatic tradition, but in the blood, horror, and vengeance found in the tragical narratives of *The Mirror for Magistrates*.

Between the bloody account of Bessus' death and the anguish of Alexander, Sackville interjects a stanza that reinforces his didactic aim and once more mentions God:

Take hede ye princes and ye prelates all
Of this outrage, which though it slepe a while
And not disclosde, as it doth seeld befall,
Yet God that suffreth silence to beguyle
Such gyltes, wherwith both earth and ayre ye file,
At last discryes them to your fowle deface,
You see the examples set before your face.
(127-33)

This stanza offers a necessary emotional pause after the swift stanzas depicting violent death. We too are somewhat breathless, and the pause to restate Sackville's intent and to reaffirm the presence of God prepares us for the account of Alexander to which Sackville devotes five stanzas — a marvelous picture, complete in itself, of the agony of a man who made a horrible mistake:

And deepely grave within your stony hartes,
The drery dewle that myghty Macedo,
With teares vnfolded wrapt in deadly smartes,
When he the death of Clitus sorowed so,
Whom erst he murdred wyth the deadly blowe
Raught in his rage vpon his frende so deare,
For which behold loe how his panges appere.

The launced spear he writhes out of the wound,
From which the purple blud spins on his face:
His heynous gylt when he returned found,
He throwes him selfe vpon the corpes alas.
And in his armes howe ofte doth he imbrace
His murdred frende? and kyssyng him in vayne,
Furth flowe the fluds of salte repentant rayne.

His frendes amazde at such a murder doen,
In feareful flockes begyn to shrynke away.
And he thereat with heapes of griefe fordoen,
Hateth him selfe, wishing his latter daye.
Nowe he him selfe perceyued in like staye,
As is the wilde beast in the desert bred,
Both dreading others and him selfe adred.

He calles for Death, and loathing lenger lyfe,
Bent to his bane, refuseth kyndely foode:
And ploungde in depth of death and dolours stryfe,
Had quelde him selfe, had not his frendes wythstoode.

Loe he that thus had shed the gylteles blud,
Though he wer Kyng and Kesar over all
Yet chose he death to guerdon death withall.

This prynce whose pyer was never vnder sonne,
Whose glystening fame the earth did overglyde,
Whych with his power welnye the world had wonne,
His bluddy handes him selfe could not abyde,
But fully bent with famine to have dyed:
The wurthy prynce deemed in his regarde,
That Death for death could be but iust rewarde.
(134-68)

This passage is surely one of the best in the poem because Sackville has been able in thirty-five lines to carry on the theme of all the previous examples — that blood begets blood, that death is a just reward for death; and the thread of violence, presenting realistic details, contains at the same time the softer emotions and the agony of a man who realizes that what is done cannot be undone. Alexander's embrace of his dead friend, the kissing, the tears, the wish to die — these are true and felt results of the act of murder. Alexander's remorse seems to be Sackville's invention, since his source for the episode, Lydgate, makes no mention of Alexander's reaction to the death. Sackville's brief switch of perspective to the witnesses of the murder — the amazed friends who shrink away from so horrible a deed — fills out a scene worthy of the best poets and, might I add, dramatists. For in this vignette about Alexander, Sackville, fusing effective external description with the reaction of lookers-on and with Alexander's believable introspection, creates a veritable dramatic scene. The distance between this scene and those that we find later in the plays of the Elizabethan dramatists is not great.

Sackville rushes from these examples of just rewards for violence and from the introspection of Alexander to the self-examination of Buckingham:

Yet we that were so drowned in the depth
Of diepe desyre to drinke the gylteles blud,
Lyke to the sulfe, with greedy lookes that lepth
Into the snare, to feede on deadly foode,
So we delyghted in the state we stoode,
Blinded so farre in all our blynded trayne
That blind we sawe not our destruction playne.
(169-75)

Here Buckingham succinctly analyzes the passion which destroys him and Richard. The drinking, we notice, continues, and this time Buckingham also drinks. The "d's" of "deep desire" and "drowned" and "depth" and "deadly" and "delyhted" lead to the "d" of "destruction." Buckingham and Richard are both wolves here, and very deep in blood. Having murdered those around them — not without some regret by Buckingham: "My heart even bleedes to tell you" — they accomplish their objective: "He crowned king, and I his chyefest Pyer." Fortune, Buckingham says, is with them; it has put in their laps the realm. This moment is for Buckingham the highest point on Fortune's wheel; from now on, he goes down, down.

The immediate result of their bloody rise is the working of conscience. The effects of a guilty conscience, vividly described, were probably taken by Sackville directly from Hall and may have influenced Shakespeare's treatment of conscience in *Richard III*. Buckingham talks of the guiltless blood that he and Richard "unjustly" shed, the heavy burdens that begin to press them, the torment that they feel, the sleepless nights and restless thoughts of a "guylty minde." Now Fortune, because conscience is at work, is called slippery — "The wheele whurles up, but strayt it whurleth downe."

The tyranny of Richard, says Buckingham, instilled fear into the hearts of all; but this fear won Richard hatred, which caused Richard himself to be beset inwardly by fear. His dread is compared with that of all tyrants, who must of necessity find that fear and unrest accompany their force. He describes the fate of Phereus, a terribly cruel tyrant, whose behavior brings to mind the Dread of the "Induction." He mentions Nero, Phalaris, Caligula, and Domitian, all notoriously cruel tyrants who were beset by fear. Richard is not less cruel than these tyrants, so cruel, says Buckingham, that "my selfe now loathde his crueltee."

From this point in the poem (line 336), Sackville begins to emphasize Buckingham's change of heart and his desire to work against Richard. Until now he has been equally guilty in Richard's rise, and his "deserved" fate has been stressed. Now the balance seems to be tipping the other way, for Buckingham recognizes the cruelty of Richard, especially in his murder of the young princes, "gylteless babes." He also recognizes the "envious frowne" of Richard, who dreads all around him, but especially Buckingham, who had helped to raise him so high. Knowing that Richard is seeking his death, the Duke has a choice — "To wurke his death or I my selfe to dye." This idea leads to a stanza-long simile:

And as the knyght in fyeld among his foes,
Beset wyth swurdes, must slaye or there be slayne:
So I alas lapt in a thousand woes,
Beholding death on every syde so playne,
I rather chose by sum slye secrete trayne
To wurke his death, and I to lyve thereby,
Than he to lyve, and I of force to dye.
(386-92)

The sense of inevitability informs the stanza; the choices of the tragic "hero" — here Buckingham the "knyght" — become limited, and the course of action becomes horribly clear.

He secretly makes plans to fight the king, raises an army, and seems confident; but Fortune, who was at his "becke," he thought, suddenly "chaunged her chere, and left me post alone." The army shrinks away in cowardly fashion, and Buckingham blames Fortune and the common people:

For such is Fortune when she lyst to frowne,
Who seemes most sure, him soonest whurles she down

O let no prynce put trust in commontie,
Nor hope in fayth of gyddy peoples mynde,
But let all noble men take hede by me,
That by the proofe to well the payne do fynde:
Loe, where is truth or trust? or what could bynde
The vayne people, but they will swarve and swaye,
As chaunce bryngs chaunge, to dryve & draw that way?
(419-27)

The strong relationship between Fortune and the people is evident: both are fickle and capricious; both change and cannot be trusted. Fortune's mutability and the crowd's inconstancy work together to help cause Buckingham's fall.

Thoughts of the giddy people, an Elizabethan commonplace, give rise to eight stanzas of historical illustration. The bookish Sackville emerges here; for his examples, some interestingly presented, tend to slow the narrative at a crucial moment in Buckingham's career. His stanzas deal with those who were ruined by the fickle mob — Camillus, Scipio, Milciades, Hannibal; and the notion of exile is the thread that ties the illustrations together. Such exile helps to accentuate the "alone" that Buckingham used in connection with his own plight; for, like his examples, Buckingham is forced into isolation by the "unstable commontye" and "bryttle Fortune." He ends the digression with a stanza filled with questions:

> Vnfrendly Fortune shal I thee nowe blame?
> Or shal I fault the fates that so ordayne?
> Or art thou love the causer of the same?
> Or crueltie her selfe doth she constrayne?
> Or on whom els alas shal I complayne?
> O trustles world I can accusen none,
> But fyckle fayth of commontye alone.
> (484-90)

These are important questions, for with them Sackville anticipates the critical problem most connected with the *Complaint* — to whom or what does one ascribe the blame for Buckingham's fall. Buckingham eliminates Fortune, the fates, and Jove (God) as the cause, and he pins the entire blame on the common people. This viewpoint is difficult to accept, but we must remember that it comes from Buckingham, not from Sackville. Buckingham, in a rage because of his betrayal and death caused by the treachery of the people and of a single friend, becomes passionate. Realizing his state of isolation — "alone" — he weeps, complains, and cries out against the most obvious cause of his fall — the cause that he is thinking of now. The questions are not the result of a reasoning process; they are the beginning of a cry for vengeance against the people, as the betrayal of Banaster crowds into his thoughts at this moment:

> And beyng thus alone, and all forsake,
> Amyd the thycke, forwandred in despayer,
> As one dismayed ne wyst what waye to take,
> Vntyll at last gan to my mynde repayer,
> A man of mine called Humfrey Banastair:
> Wherewyth me feeling much recomforted,
> In hope of succour to his house I fled.
> (512-18)

The "alone" and the "thycke" help us to recall the situation of the narrator of the "Induction" who is also in a sorrowful state and is about to find company on a journey to Hell. Buckingham, to avoid aloneness, seeks out the friend whose treachery leads him to hell; for we can never forget that a ghost is talking:

For by this wretche I beyng strayt betrayed,
To one Iohn Mitton, shiriffe of Shropshire then,
All sodaynely was taken, and conuayed
To Salisbury, wyth rout of harnest men,
Vnto Kyng Rychard there encamped then:
Fast by the citye with a myghtye hoste
Withouten doome where head and lyfe I lost.
(533-39)

His narrative ends suddenly — as suddenly as the quick betrayal, as suddenly as the changes of Fortune and people, as suddenly as ax separates head from body. When Buckingham's monologue ends, we switch to the poet-narrator who informs us that "Ded fel he downe: and we in woful feare / Stood mazed when he would to lyef revert." This statement is the first direct reaction of the narrator to Buckingham. Until this point, the responses were all Buckingham's; now the listeners, Sackville and Sorrow, must be heard.

The stillness of Buckingham and the deathly quality of his swoon bring forth the poem's most beautiful description:

Mydnyght was cum, and every vitall thyng
With swete sound slepe theyr weary lyms dyd rest,
The beastes were still, the lytle byrdes that syng,
Nowe sweetely slept besides theyr mothers brest:
The olde and all were shrowded in theyr nest.
The waters calme, the cruel seas did ceas,
The wuds, the fyeldes & all thinges held theyr peace.

The golden stars wer whyrlde amyd theyr race,
And on the earth did laugh wyth twinkling lyght,
When eche thing nestled in his restyng place,
Forgat dayes payne with pleasure of the nyght:
The Hare had not the greedy houndes in sight,
The fearful Dear of death stoode not in doubt,
The Patrydge drept not of the Falcons foote.

The ougly Beare nowe mynded not the stake,
Nor how the cruell mastyues do hym tear,
The stag laye still vnroused from the brake,
The fomy boar feard not the hunters spear.
All thing was still in desert, bush and brear.
With quyet hart now from their trauailes rest,
Soundly they slept in midst of all their rest.
(547-67)

This poetry is pure, sweet, smooth, and golden. The rhythms lull; the tone is solemn. These stanzas could stand alone as an important contribution to English poetry; but, at the same time, they are perfectly suited to the *Complaint* as a whole. The treachery of Banaster, following closely upon the treachery of the common people, has led to the death of Buckingham. The thought of his death causes Buckingham to swoon, to enter briefly a deathly state in the world of the dead. The layers of death are felt — for Buckingham is a dead man speaking; his temporary dying in death adds to the terror and mystery. The words on midnight, so calm and sweet, are a brilliant contrast to the man-made treachery of the preceding stanzas. The nourishment that comes from the "mothers brest," the whirling of the golden stars — how different from the whirling of Fortune's wheel — the stars' "twinkling" light, the quiet heart — all are welcome reliefs from the previous cruelty. We are briefly reminded of this cruelty in the bear-baiting image, for the world that Buckingham presents in his narrative is the world of dogs tearing at bears. No other lines are needed, I believe, to testify to Sackville's poetic gifts and narrative sense.

Buckingham's swoon leads to twitching and then to rage. The sighs he heaves are stormy and swelling. The tears he sheds are rivers. His eyes are blood red, and he froths at the mouth. His features and actions cause the narrator's limbs to tremble with fear. When Buckingham speaks again, he hurls raging curses against Banaster:

> Thou Banaster, gaynst thee I clepe and call
> Vnto the Gods, that they iust vengeaunce take
> On thée, thy bloud, thy stayned stocke and all;
> O Iove, to thée aboue the rest I make
> My humble playnt, guyde me that what I speake,
> May be thy wyll vpon thys wretche to fall,
> On thée Banastar, wretch of wretches all.
> (638-44)

He is looking for vengeance, and we recall the "blood will have blood" stanzas in the poem's beginning. The curse against Banaster lasts for eleven stanzas, in which Sackville the poet once again presents a series of questions, this time indicating "the unsuerty in this life":

To this did I even from thy tender youth
Witsafe to bryng thée vp? dyd I herfore
Beleve the oath of thy vndoubted trouth?
Aduaunce thée vp, and trust thée evermore?
By trusting thée that I should dye therefore?
O wretche, and wurse than wretche, what shal I say?
But cleap and curse gaynst thee and thine for aye.
(659-65)

We feel Buckingham's disillusionment with the man he had helped advance, just as we noticed previously his disgust with that other man he had helped become a king, Richard. The questions point to the slipperiness of man's affections and to the self-seeking nature of man.

The curse becomes most devastating when Buckingham includes Banaster's children:

Yet shall not death delyuer thee so soone
Out of thy woes, so happye shalt thou not bee:
But to the eternall Ioue this is my boone,
That thou may liue thine eldest sonne to see
Reft of his wits, and in a fowle bores stye
To ende his dayes in rage and death distrest,
A wurthy tumbe where one of thyne should rest.

And after this, yet pray I more, thou may
Thy second sonne sée drowned in a dyke,
And in such sorte to close his latter daye,
As heard or seen earst hath not bene the lyke:
Ystrangled in a puddle not so deepe
As halfe a foote, that such hard losse of lyfe,
So cruelly chaunst, may be thy greater gryefe.

And not yet shall thy hugie sorrowes cease,
Ioue shal not so withholde his wrath fro thée,
But that thy plagues may more and more encreas,
Thou shalt still lyve, that thou thy selfe mayst sée
Thy deare doughter stroken with leprosye:
That she that earst was all thy hole delyght,
Thou now mayst loath to haue her cum in sight.

And after that, let shame and sorrowes gryefe
Feede furth thy yeares continually in wo,
That thou mayest live in death, and dye in lyef,

> And in this sorte forewayld and wearyed so,
> Al length thy ghost to parte thy body fro:
> This pray I Iove, and wyth this latter breath,
> Vengeaunce I aske vpon my cruell death.
> (686-714)

The fate of Banaster's children was indeed the fate that Buckingham presents here; Buckingham is prophetic, but Sackville was working with hindsight, helped by Hall and some ballads.

The powerful curse, which must remind us of Margaret's utterances in *Richard III,* causes Buckingham to be completely spent. He strives again with death in death, he becomes pale and cold, he is silent, and then he sighs stormily. Finally he utters the questions that lead to mental imbalance:

> Ah where am I, what thing, or whence is this?
> Who reft my wyts? or howe do I thus lye?
> My lims do quake, my thought agasted is,
> Why sygh I so? Or wherevnto do I
> Thus grovle on the ground?
> (729-33)

This piling up of questions is Sackville's vehicle to indicate confusion of character and the fragile line between reason and passion. Returning to reason, he tells his listeners to "thinke on my death," to "take hede by me." He told his story to teach, and once again it is to Fortune, "false Fortune," that he directs his attention. The last two stanzas of the poem, like the poem's beginning, deal with Fortune and with Sackville's intent:

> For of my byrth, my blud was of the best,
> Fyrst borne an Earle, than duke by due discent:
> To swinge the sway in court amonge the rest,
> Dame Fortune me her rule most largely lent:
> And kynd with corage so my corps had blent,
> That loe on whom but me dyd she most smyle?
> And whom but me lo, dyd she most begyle?
>
> Now hast thou heard the whole of my vnhap,
> My chaunce, my chaunge, the cause of all my care:
> In wealth and wo, how Fortune dyd me wrap,
> With world at will to win me to her snare.
> Byd kynges, byd kesars, by all states beware,

> And tell them this from me that tryed it true.
> Who reckles rules, right soone may hap to rue.
> (764-77)

The high man of good birth and blood, because of smiling beguiling Fortune, has been brought low. His last three lines are a direct warning to magistrates to rule wisely — the purpose for presenting his complaint, and the ostensible reason for the presence of this poem in *The Mirror for Magistrates.*

These last lines have been crucial in discussions of Sackville's intent and in considerations of the particular reasons for Buckingham's fall. The recklessness of rulers, to many a critic, is not Sackville's emphasis throughout the poem. Willard Farnham pins Buckingham's fall squarely on Fortune,[3] not on his recklessness; R. G. Howarth says that Buckingham "had committed no moral fault," but was beguiled by Fortune;[4] Paul Bacquet, more sensibly, sees Buckingham as a victim of both Fortune and Divine Justice, one who is paying for his sins;[5] and Howard Baker considers the poem's "moral significance" to be "obscure."[6] We remember that Buckingham himself discounted Fortune and God as the causes of his fall in favor of the common people's inconstancy.

The existence of these differing interpretations raises important questions. Is the poem fuzzy on the question of responsibility? Does Sackville intend to point a lesson but in fact does not? (We did, after all, find that the didactic intent of the "Induction" was lost in the brilliant descriptions of that mood piece.) The poem has been called diffuse and rambling, and is it so because the question of responsibility is left vague, or because no one idea or purpose seems to be directing the poem? These questions are crucial, because the answers point directly to the quality of Sackville's art.

It is a temptation to say that the differing interpretations stem from Sackville's intent to build mystery into the poem, that the vagueness is purposeful — what we can say about *Hamlet,* for example. We do find a great number of questions in the poem, and my commentary has pinpointed most of these. The questions help to produce what we could call "a baffled tone"; the interrogative mood is surely working on our responses. The questions touch on many issues and seem to produce an atmosphere of uncertainty, but this atmosphere hovers *around* the central idea of tragic responsibility and retribution; it does not make the idea vague. The poem does not lack a vigorous kind of causal logic, for the last words clearly summarize what Sackville has been saying throughout and are the natural outcome of all that came before.

The notion of Fortune does tend, however, to obscure the problem. Fortune, as an idea, had an extraordinary vogue for the Middle Ages and the Elizabethan Age, and the influence of Boethius's *De Consolatione* was of the greatest importance in the popularization of the idea. King Alfred had translated Boethius; Medieval schools diffused the doctrine of the philosopher who was called the "Christian Seneca." Chaucer, who translated Boethius, made significant use of the idea of Fortune in *Troilus and Cressida* and in some of his tales. Queen Elizabeth translated certain passages in Boethius; and Sackville, part of Elizabeth's court and a great admirer of Chaucer, also planned to translate his work.

The Boethian Fortune was a popular concept which Medieval and Elizabethan writers understood and used. Yet, despite the many commentaries on the idea, its exact relationship to man's free will and individual responsibility remains a source of difficulty. It is an idea, a concept, that expresses what happens to every man. The idea is depicted as a goddess, but the Elizabethan did not believe in goddesses; he believed in the *idea* of Fortune, which was closely linked to his belief in Christianity and to the notion of a high Providential design. The role of Fortune, those things that happen to men by chance, is part of a larger scheme. Fortune, however, is not Destiny, which is the working of Providence in particular points in a man's life, but which itself is surmounted by the free will of man.[7]

Keeping Boethius's idea of Fortune and Providence clearly in mind, we can never say that a tragic fall is totally caused by either chance or destiny. The fall is caused by man's transgression; the tragic hero is a victim of himself. His failure may come about because of his desire for fame or wealth or physical pleasure or some other worldly satisfaction; when so possessed, he thereby loses his freedom and *becomes* a slave of Fortune; the becoming is his own doing. Once he has succumbed to his desire, once his reason is abandoned, he becomes subject to Fortune, and his doom is inevitable. In this way Fortune operates in Chaucerian tragedy, and in Sackville's tragical narrative, the *Complaint.* These ideas on individual responsibility, Fortune, and God's justice are connected in the Elizabethan mind without having the formality of a strict theory; but the connection is there.

Buckingham's complaint presents all the conventional qualities of Fortune, and he cries out against the goddess, but his own responsibility for his actions is emphasized throughout. He "consented" to the killings that led Richard III to the top; he was "joined" to Richard in his tyranny; he helped drink guiltless blood; and he talks of his fall as "deserved." That the fear and death of tyrants are brought on by their own cruelty was the subject of the many stanzas of historical illustration. The Revenge idea, which pervades the poem and reaches its climax in the curse against Banaster, depends on individual responsibility. Revenge is essentially an act of retribution for an individual's action. Buckingham is a man of high station, fortunate in his birth and blood, but his ambition for his tyrant king and his cruel actions make him subject to Fortune and change. When Fortune turns her wheel, he goes down, and doom is inevitable. His world becomes smaller; his men — the common people — desert; he is "alone"; he must wander in despair, like the exiles of the past. He can turn to one man only, and this man betrays him.

That Buckingham has sinned, however, does not make him an unsympathetic character. Sackville forces us to pity the man, for Buckingham recognizes his mistake, tries to destroy the villainous Richard, is betrayed by those closest to him, protests against the very changes in life that all men experience, and tells his story as a warning for others. The reader is in tune with his cry against the world's uncertainty, and the reader understands as well that all men are essentially sinners.

The poem contains a network of implications stemming from a number of themes. But these themes and the important ideas in the poem — Fortune, Destiny, God — are connected by Sackville's overriding purpose, of which he never loses sight: to teach, to show, that a high man, when he allows his passion and ambition to rule him, when he becomes a tyrant, will cause Fortune's wheel to turn and will leave God's grace, will trigger fear in his own mind and hatred in others, and will bring on his own death; for blood will have blood.

The poem is not merely a grab-bag of different ideas joined only by the man moaning them. The principle of unity in the poem is strong, for all of these ideas are vitally connected to the idea of mutability — "the sundry chaunges that in earth we fynde," as the "Induction" states it; "the unsuerty in this life," as Buckingham expresses it. Mutability, however, springs from man's action. If it did not, then what would be the purpose of presenting a mirror to warn and to teach magistrates?

With the emphasis on blood and death, the *Complaint* suggests to us a powerful sense of mortality. With its stress on Fortune and mutability, it tells us of the instability of human ambition. With its many questions, it points to the mystery of life. And with its preoccupation with Justice — the "deserved fall," the deserved deaths — it points to a responsibility and retribution that are clear and unmistakable.

The poem deserves a better critical reception than it has received, for it has intrinsic worth — unity, harmony, poetic excellences, sustained tone, moral significance. Moreover, its themes of Revenge, Fortune, and Retribution, together with its depiction of a sympathetic, tragic hero, significantly anticipate the greatness of Elizabethan tragedy.

CHAPTER 6

Gorboduc

STUDENTS of English drama have always been aware of *Gorboduc,* if not always ready to praise its artistic worth. The play finds its respected place with other landmarks in the history of literature which receive approbation because of the historical advance they make but which have little else to recommend them. *Gorboduc,* as a work of art, has been condemned by those who have read and not read it. Homer Watt's assertion that, for most students of English literature, *Gorboduc* is "synonymous with all that is dull, pedantic, stiff, and inartistic in the early Elizabethan drama"[1] is correct. David Daiches represents most literary historians when he states that *Gorboduc* is "sententious, rhetorical, and supremely dull" and that, although it is historically important, "it is a play that nobody today would read for pleasure."[2]

The play did enjoy a popularity in its own time, and Sir Philip Sidney's praise of *Gorboduc* is an important and much quoted touchstone of Renaissance criticism:

> Our Tragedies and Comedies (not without cause cried out against), observing rules neyther of honest civilitie nor of skilful Poetrie, excepting *Gorboduck* (againe, I say, of those that I have seene), which notwithstanding, as it is full of stately speeches and well sounding Phrases, clyming to the height of *Seneca* his stile, and as full of notable moralitie, which it doth most delightfully teach, and so obtayne the very end of Poesie, yet in troth it is very defectious in the circumstaunces, which greeveth mee, because it might not remaine as an exact model of all Tragedies. For it is faulty both in place and time, the two necessary companions of all corporall actions. For where the stage should alwaies represent but one place, and the uttermost time presupposed in it should be, both by *Aristotles* precept and common reason, but one day, there is both many days, and many places, inartificially imagined. But if it be so in *Gorboduck,* how much more in al the rest?[3]

Sidney, the champion of Classicism, finds much to praise in *Gorboduc;* but he also expresses some disappointment with the play's lack of adherence to the Aristotelian unities. The play fell into oblivion for about a century before Dryden refers to it in a dedication to *The Rival Ladies* and before another Classicist, Alexander Pope, following the lead of Thomas Rymer, records his praise of the play: "The writers of the succeeding age might have improved as much in other respects, by copying from him [Sackville] a propriety in the sentiments, and dignity in the sentences, and an unaffected perspicuity of style, which are so essential to tragedy, and which all the succeeding poets, not excepting Shakespeare himself, either little understood, or perpetually neglected."[4]

From the late nineteenth century to the present, *Gorboduc* has received treatment in histories of English drama. Though applauded for its contribution to the development of drama, it is, as we have noted, universally condemned as uninteresting. Charles Lamb perhaps best expresses the usual attitude toward *Gorboduc:* ". . . the style of this old play is stiff and cumbersome, like the dresses of its times. There may be flesh and blood underneath, but we cannot get at it."[5] The purpose of this chapter is to "get at it" — to discuss the intrinsic worth of the play as well as to examine the reasons for its importance to the history of English drama.

I *Date, Performance, Printing*

Gorboduc was first performed in 1561 at a Christmas celebration before the gentlemen of the Inner Temple, one of the four great Inns of Court. Productions at the Inns of Court, although amateur and not meant for the general public, tended to be lavish and were seen by families of the highest rank. When the play was successful enough to be repeated before Queen Elizabeth at Whitehall on January 18, this performance was recorded in the diary of Henry Machyn: "The xviij day of January was a play in the quen ('s) hall at Westmynster by the gentyll-men of the Tempull, and after a grett maske, for ther was a grett skaffold in the hall, with grett tryhumpe as has bene sene; and the morow after the skaffold was taken done."[6] Machyn's emphasis on the spectacle reinforces our belief that the students of the Inns of Court delighted in elaborate entertainments and in splendid pomp for their celebration of Christmas.

Gorboduc was written for the entertainment of students by two future statesmen, Thomas Norton and Thomas Sackville, and the authors had no intention of publishing the play for posterity. The two performances — these are the only ones recorded — were of a private nature; and the play might have remained merely an item on a list or a jotting in a diary had not a copy of the play been sold by some unknown man to the printer William Griffith. The pirated edition of *Gorboduc* was issued from Griffith's press on September 22, 1565, with this title-page: "The/Tragedie of Gorboduc/Where of three Actes were wrytten by/Thomas Nortone, and the two laste by/Thomas Sackuyle. Sett forthe as the same was shewed before the/Quenes most excellent Maiestie, in her highnes/Court of Whitehall, the .XVIIJ day of January,/*Anno Domini* .1561. By the Gentlemen/of Thynner Temple in London."

According to John Day, the printer of the second and authorized edition, Sackville and Norton knew nothing about the 1565 edition and were, in fact, not in London at the time. In a letter "to the reader," Day criticizes Griffith for printing an "excedingly corrupted" — which it is not — edition of the play; but we can be thankful that Griffith saved the play for us. The second, authorized edition of 1570 has the following title-page: "The Tragidie of Ferrex/and Porrex,/set forth without addition or alte-/ration but altogether as the same was shewed/on stage before the Quuenes Maiestie,/about nine yeares past, *vz.* the/xviij day of Ianuarie 1561./by the gentlemen of the/Inner Temple Seen and allowed &c."

The play had one more edition during the authors' lifetime, this printed by Edward Allde in 1590. The title-page reads: "The Tragedie of Gorboduc, whereof three Actes were written by Thomas Norton, and the two last by Thomas Sackuyle. Set forth as the same was shewed before the Queenes most excellent majesty, in her highnes Court of Whitehall, by the Gentlemen of the Inner Temple." This edition was printed together with John Lydgate's tract, *The Serpent of Division* (1400), so that once again we find Lydgate and Sackville joined together, as they were when *The Mirror for Magistrates* was projected as a continuation of Lydgate's *The Fall of Princes*.

II *Authorship*

The authorship of *Gorboduc* has been the object of much scholarly debate. The play is a collaboration, as the early editions indicate; but Norton's share has been questioned and a brief review of the life of Thomas Norton is helpful in making a determination about his part in writing the play. At the writing of *Gorboduc,* Norton, like Sackville, was a young man concerned about the political affairs of the Elizabethan reign. He was Sackville's senior by four years, having been born in 1532; and he had entered as a student in the Inner Temple in 1555, two years before he became a member of the Parliament of 1558, of which Sackville was also a member.

Whereas Sackville was a conservative aristocrat upholding the conventional attitudes of his day, Norton was devoted to the Puritan cause — and this cause colored his thinking and activity during his entire life. His stepfather, with whom he lived for a short period of time, was Edward Whitchurch, the Calvinist printer, at whose home an active group of English Puritans congregated; and he also first originated the general scheme for *The Mirror for Magistrates.* John Day, the printer of the authorized 1570 edition of *Gorboduc,* was one of Norton's Puritan friends. Norton's first wife was the daughter of Archbishop Cranmer, and his second wife was the archbishop's cousin. Norton in 1561 translated John Calvin's *Institutes of the Christian Religion,* and a year later he contributed twenty-eight psalms to the Sternhold and Hopkins metrical version of the Psalter that had been printed ten years earlier by Whitchurch. At Oxford, which Norton entered in 1565 and left in 1569 with a master of arts degree, his Calvinist spirit led to the issuing of polemical pamphlets against the Catholics. During the years in which he served as member of Parliament and as Remembrancer to his native city of London, he engaged in persecution of the Papists. So zealous was he and so cruel was his action that his reputation suffered, and he was imprisoned in the Tower briefly in 1583. He died in 1584.[7]

This brief summary of Norton's career indicates that his main interest was politics and polemics, that he had literary interests, that his political path must have crossed Sackville's, that he had firm connections with both the printer of the authorized version of *Gorboduc,* Day, and with the original conceiver of *The Mirror for Magistrates,* Whitchurch. Since the political ideas he expressed in Parliament are very close to those expressed in *Gorboduc,* since he was actively concerned with the succession, and since he is named as co-author in the three editions of the play that appear in Sackville's lifetime, it is very difficult to reject his part in the collaboration.

Nonetheless, his claim has been rejected by some. Thomas Warton, the first to assert that *Gorboduc* was the work of one man, Thomas Sackville, does not trust the external evidence, which he finds "suspicious"; and he, therefore, relies upon "the force of internal evidence" to establish his view. He dismisses Norton's claim with this assertion: "Thomas Norton's poetry is of a very different and a subordinate cast: and if we may judge from his share in our metrical psalmody, he seems to have been much more properly qualified to shine in the miserable mediocrity of Sternhold's stanza, and to write spiritual rhymes for the solace of his illuminated brethren, than to reach the bold and impassioned elevations of tragedy."[8] That Norton's contributions to the Psalms show none of the poetic excellences that we may find in *Gorboduc* cannot be disputed, but this fact is surely not substantial enough to dismiss Norton's claim, especially because the task of translating the psalms is a difficult one and cannot be the most accurate measure of a poet.

Warton's view is shared by many editors and scholars, who also find that the play is too uniform to be the work of more than one man; but none has presented compelling reasons for denying Norton's claim. *Gorboduc* does seem uniform in conception, intent, and prosody; but this uniformity is not unusual when we consider that Sackville and Norton were closely associated in public interests; were following similar models; were working with a new medium for drama, blank verse; and were interested, despite their ideological differences, in expressing similar political ideas in *Gorboduc.* Subtler differences in expression, style, and tone can be discerned between roughly the first three and the last two acts of the play; but, for the most part, the play is *one,* the product of a close and successful collaboration. In short, all of the external evidence favors Norton's claim and the internal evidence — the metrical differences and differences in expression in the first three acts — support it.[9]

The exact nature of any collaboration is difficult to determine; for, even after a battery of tests and an assortment of contemporary testimonials assign specific scenes to specific dramatists, we are never certain about the working habits of the collaborators. Did each oversee the other's work? Did they revise together? Did they discuss before writing? Did one rewrite the whole? Did one act as mentor; the other, as disciple? In the collaboration which produced *Gorboduc,* we are on comparatively safe ground about the division of labor; but the product, the entire play, must be considered the work of both men; and the merits and faults of the entire play must be attributed to each. Sackville, therefore, must be considered responsible not only for the last two acts, which he probably wrote alone, but for the intent, design, and execution of the whole.

III *Political Intent*

Not surprisingly, *Gorboduc* expresses political ideas. The play is written by two men actively concerned with the political life of their country; it is presented before an intelligent audience interested in political matters; it is performed before the Queen; and its aim is to instruct Queen Elizabeth about specific political issues. Commentators on *Gorboduc,* who have stressed its political intent, pinpoint the play's specific relevance to the reign of Elizabeth; and one of the major concerns of the English people throughout Elizabeth's reign was the uncertain succession. Elizabeth's claim to the throne was legitimate, since it was based on Henry VIII's will and sanctioned by Parliament. But there were claimants to the crown; and these, of course, could be potential successors if Elizabeth left no heir. The two chief claimants were Lady Catherine Grey and Mary, Queen of Scots; the former, because Henry VIII's will placed the Suffolk house in line for succession; the latter, because the Tudor female line had to be considered if Henry's will was ignored. Lady Catherine was strongly favored by Protestants; Mary, by Catholics. Most of the English people had no desire to replace Elizabeth with anyone; but they were concerned, understandably so, that the succession be settled to avoid the chaos that would come if rival claimants divided the realm; for the civil wars of the fifteenth century were not forgotten. Elizabeth could have eased the tensions of her subjects by either marrying and bearing children who would be the natural heirs or by definitely naming her successor. She did neither.

Elizabeth's first Parliament, that of 1558, of which both Sackville and Norton were members, petitioned her to marry for the good of the realm. Her answer was that she would not marry and that it would be for her "sufficient, that a marble stone shall declare that a Queen, have reigned such a time, lived and died a virgin." Between the dissolution of this first Parliament and the opening of the second one in January, 1563, Elizabeth had still not made an effort to settle the succession — even though in the interim she had been dangerously ill with smallpox and Mary Stuart had landed in Scotland to make demands on the crown. The Parliament of 1563 is the one most commentators on the play discuss, even though it was convened a year after *Gorboduc* was performed. This Parliament, also including Sackville and Norton as members, again petitioned Elizabeth to marry and to limit the succession; and Norton probably was the author of this petition.[10]

In this interim between Parliaments, *Gorboduc* was performed with the Queen as part of its second audience. As these parliamentary activities indicate, the establishment of the succession was of great importance to Elizabethans; and it was certainly a debated topic when *Gorboduc* was performed. The play addresses itself to the succession and also presents other political ideas which stem from the discussion on succession.[11]

The political purpose of *Gorboduc* can be demonstrated clearly by looking at a few of the many political speeches in the play. Of course, the plea for establishment of succession is the most pervasive political argument. Hermon, Ferrex's evil adviser, could be talking directly to Queen Elizabeth when he says:

> "Wise men do not so hang on passing state
> "Of present princes, chiefely in their age,
> "But they will further cast their reaching eye
> "To viewe and weye the times and reignes to come."
> (II,1,126-29)[12]

That a kingdom could be destroyed when division occurs is the gist of Eubulus' early speech:

> To parte your realme vnto my lordes your sonnes
> I thinke not good for you, ne yet for them,
> But worste of all for this our natiue lande.
> Within one land one single rule is best:
> Diuided reignes do make diueded hartes,
> But peace preserues the countrey and the prince.
> (I,2,256-61)

The explanation to the dumb show preceding the last act states (italics mine): "Hereby was signified tumults, rebellions, armes and ciuill wares to follow: as fell in the realme of Great Brittayne, which by the space of fiftie yeares and more continued in ciuill warre betwene the nobilitie after the death of King Gorboduc and of his issues, *for want of certayne limitacion in sucession of the crowne,* till the time of Dunwallo Molmutius, who reduced the land to monarchie." "The Argument of the Tragedie" contains these words: ". . . and afterwardes, for want of issue of the prince, whereby the succession of the crowne became vncertaine, they fell to ciuill warre, in which both they and many of their issues were slaine, and the land for a long time almost desolate and miserable wasted." Eubulus follows his description of the horrors of civil war with these words:

> This, this ensues when noble-men do faile
> In loyall trouth, and subiectes will be kinges.
> And this doth growe when, loe, vnto the prince
> Whom death or sodeine happe of life bereaues
> No certaine heire remaines — such certaine heire
> As not all-onely is the rightfull heire
> But to the realme is so make knowen to be,
> And trouth therby vested in subiectes hartes
> To owe fayth there where right is knowen to rest.
> (V,2,244-52)

The fear of a foreign ruler is related to the notion of succession; the hope was that Elizabeth would avoid marrying that foreigner, Philip of Spain, and that Mary Stuart would not succeed. The play stresses a "native line" and "a former lawe" — favoring, it seems. Lady Catherine Grey. In the play, although Fergus, Duke of Albany, has no claim to the throne (since he is considered to be a foreign prince), he is able to take advantage of a chaotic time to gather strength and to make his forceful bid for the crown — one which leads to bloodshed and more chaos.

Sackville and Norton indicate by means of the last speech of Eubulus that Parliament must play an important role in questions of succession. Eubulus stresses that Parliament, often racked by divisions, must have a guiding force, the king. The king must summon parliament and clearly indicate his heirs, for only in this way could order be enforced in the commonwealth:

> No, no; then Parliament should haue bene holden,
> And certeine heires appointed to the crowne,
> To stay the title of established right,
> And in the people plant obedience
> While yet the prince did liue, whose name and power
> By lawfull sommons and authoritie
> Might make a Parliament to be of force,
> And might haue set the state in quiet stay.
> (V,2,264-71)

That kings — and the Queen of the audience — are divinely appointed to rule is clearly established in the play, as is the notion that the king should not be resisted. Both of these ideas are commonplaces of Elizabethan political thought, but the latter has been challenged. Sara R. Watson asserts that Norton, a radical Puritan, evidently knew and believed in the teachings of Christopher Goodman, author of *How Superior Powers Oght to be Obeyd,* a tract which argues for tyrannicide when a king is oppressive. If kings do not follow natural law, Goodman argues, they forfeit the right to receive obedience. Watson uses as her evidence this statement by the parasitic Hermon:

> Know ye that lust of kingdomes hath no law:
> The goddes do beare and well allow in kinges
> The thinges [that] they abhorre in rascall routes.
> "When kinges on slender quarrells runne to warres,
> "And then, in cruell and vnkindely wise,
> "Commaund theftes, rapes, murders of innocentes,
> "The spoile of townes, ruines of mighty realmes, —
> "Thinke you such princes do suppose them-selues
> "Subiect to lawes of Kinde and feare of gods?"
> Murders and violent theftes in priuate men
> Are hainous crimes, and full of foule reproch;
> Yet none offence, but deckt with glorious name
> Of noble conquestes, in the handes of kinges.
> (II,1,143-55)

Since this advice is followed and causes chaos, Watson argues against its acceptance. To be sure, the terms of Hermon's speech are presented too grossly and seem evil, but the sentiments upholding the divinity of kings and the necessity for obedience by subjects cannot be challenged. Hermon's advice is supported by the words of Gwenard, who uses healthier terms:

> Shall subiectes dare with force
> To worke reuenge vpon their princes fact?
> Admit the worst that may (as sure in this
> The deede was fowle, the queene to slay her sonne),
> Shall yet the subiect seeke to take the sworde,
> Arise agaynst his lord, and slay his king?
> (V,1,18-22)

And Eubulus, the spokesman for the dramatists, expresses the commonplace in this way:

> [That no cause serues wherby the subiect maye
> Call to accompt the doynges of his prince,
> Much lesse in bloode by sworde to worke reuenge,
> No more then maye the hande cut of the heade.
> In acte nor speache, no, not in secrete thoughte,
> The subiect maye rebell against his lorde,
> Or iudge of him that sittes in Ceasars seate,
> With grudging minde to damne those he mislikes.]
> Though kinges forget to gouerne as they ought,
> Yet subiectes must obey as they are bounde.
> (V,1,42-51)

It is tempting to separate Norton and Sackville in these opinions and to consider Norton the forward-looking Puritan who upholds tyrannicide under certain conditions while Sackville would be the conservative who rejects it under any circumstance. But the play, despite collaboration, is a whole; and the total impression supports the Elizabethan commonplace that subjects are "bound" to obey their sovereign lord.

In all of these political matters, especially in the grave problem of succession, Sackville and Norton were obviously tempted to present a sermon; and they succumbed to the temptation. The idea repeated throughout *Gorboduc* is that rulers should listen to the good advice of their statesmen. Gorboduc's first words express this important notion:

> My lords, whose graue aduise and faithful aide
> Haue long vpheld my honour and my realme,
> And brought me to this age from tender yeres,
> Guidying so great estate with great renowme,
> Nowe more importeth mee than erst to vse
> Your fayth and wisedome.
> (I,2,1-6)

At the play's end, Eubulus's summary of the tragic happenings in the story contains the cause of the tragedy — failure to listen to good advice:

> Hereto it commes when kinges will not consent
> To graue aduise, but followe wilfull will.
> This is the end when in fonde princes hartes
> Flattery preuailes, and sage rede hath no place.
> (V,2,234-37)

And between these two statements the idea is repeated by various characters and is visually presented in the dumb show preceding the second act, in which the king accepts from a flattering counselor the poison in a gold cup instead of wine in a glass from a faithful counselor. Sackville and Norton never let the Queen forget that she should listen to the good advice of the writers of this play and, by extension, to the petitioners of the first Parliament who continue to urge her to act on the succession.[13]

That Sackville and Norton are addressing themselves in *Gorboduc* to specific contemporary political problems cannot be disputed. But the tendency on the part of many critics to stress only the immediate political issues has caused them to slur the play's artistic worth and to narrow the play's political range. It should be emphasized that the political ideas expressed in *Gorboduc,* although directed to a particular situation, have wider application. Swart provides a necessary antidote to the tendency to make the political aim more and more specific by stating that most of the political passages in *Gorboduc* reflect "a general theory of statecraft."[14] And Ernest Talbert upholds Swart's view by demonstrating with substantial supporting evidence that *Gorboduc* expresses commonplaces of contemporary sixteenth-century thought. Especially important is Talbert's observation that "Elizabethan political thought was, in a very real sense, thought rather than theory. Statements that in their logical extensions into a theory might seem to contradict one another could exist very comfortably together.[15]

Both Swart and Talbert have a wider concept of the politics of the play and allow us to see *Gorboduc* more clearly as an artistic contribution. They have helped to offset the kind of approach represented by the first scholar to discuss the play's political import, L. H. Courtney, who states that *Gorboduc* "is rather a political argument than a simple tragedy."[16] The terms "argument" and "tragedy" need not be mutually exclusive. In fact, S. F. Johnson has demonstrated convincingly that the play's political purpose has widened the range of the tragic experience and has allowed the play to approach the Shakespearean mode of tragedy.[17] By way of summary, it is important to stress that the political element in *Gorboduc* is very important and that the dramatists have a political intent in writing the play, but that the play's politics are general as well as specific and that the political intent does not negate the other elements which are usually associated with dramatic art.

IV *Sources*

The political nature of *Gorboduc* and its relationship to contemporary British affairs led Sackville and Norton to choose a story from British legendary history. In resorting to their own country's history — to us, mythical or legendary; to the Elizabethans, factual — the dramatists presented the first of many English dramas based on the chronicles of Britain; therefore, *Gorboduc* has the distinction of being the first English chronicle play in our language. The ultimate source for *Gorboduc* and for all chronicle accounts of the Gorboduc story is Geoffrey of Monmouth's *Historia Regum Britanniae.* Gorboduc, supposedly living in the seventh century before Christ, was the sixteenth king descended from Brute, the great-grandson of Aeneas, who founded New Troy, or London. (King Lear was the eighth and King Arthur the most illustrious of the line.) Geoffrey of Monmouth, a monk of the twelfth century, was the first to record the story of Gorboduc and his sons; and the later chronicles, which follow Geoffrey's narrative argument, change only some names and some details.

Geoffrey tells of King Gorbogudo who has two sons, Ferrex and Porrex, who quarrel over the succession when their father gets old. Porrex plans to kill Ferrex, who escapes to France. With the help of Suardus, King of France, Ferrex returns to his kingdom and is defeated and killed by Porrex. The mother, Widen, who loved Ferrex best, avenges her older son by tearing the sleeping Porrex to pieces with the help of her women. A long civil war follows, the kingdom is divided among five kings, and finally reunited by Dunwallo Molmutius.

Because the story remains essentially the same in the later chronicles and because the play, since it is a play and not a chronicle, changes the story for dramatic purposes, it is difficult to determine the direct source of *Gorboduc.* Watt believes that Grafton's *Chronicle* is the immediate source;[18] Swart favors Fabyon's *New Chronicles of England and France.*[19] To pinpoint the direct source so precisely leads to difficulties since Grafton and Fabyon are similar in all the important details of the story, especially in recording the flight to France by Ferrex and the cutting to pieces of Porrex by his mother — both details not found in *Gorboduc.* Bacquet, who presents the most thorough discussion of sources,[20] indicates deficiencies in both Watt and Swart; and he sensibly suggests that the dramatists were not necessarily limited to one source.

When Sackville and Norton wrote *Gorboduc,* they turned to the English chronicles for a native British "historical" story. Any one chronicle — Geoffrey of Monmouth or Hardyng or Higden or Fabyon or Grafton — could have supplied them with the main line of the story; all of them could have been used. One other possible source should be mentioned, if only to be dismissed — the Theban story of Eteocles and Polynices; for Sackville and Norton were undoubtedly acquainted with the Theban cycle through their reading of Seneca. The Senecan story of the two sons of Oedipus resembles the story of the two sons of Gorboduc in that a civil war is caused by the rivalry of brothers. The differences between the stories are so many, not only in narrative detail but in tone, that it seems improbable that Sackville and Norton went directly to Seneca; but echoes of the story may have played some part in the writing of *Gorboduc.*[21] The Senecan influence on *Gorboduc* is important, but not because Seneca provides the specific idea of sibling rivalry, an idea as old as Cain and Abel.

V *Senecan Influence*

It is difficult to find a study of *Gorboduc* that does not deal with the influence of Seneca. Too few discussions have avoided the danger of overstating the case for or against Senecan influence; too few have clearly confronted the nature of the influence. We must state at the outset that *Gorboduc,* like many Elizabethan tragedies, was indeed influenced by Seneca. Seneca, a dramatist and a thinker to be reckoned with, was for the Elizabethan *the* Classical dramatist — the writer who brought tragedy to its highest peak. Since almost all Elizabethans were unfamiliar with the Greek dramatists, from whom Seneca took his inspiration, they had no standard for comparison — thereby making Seneca the only model for tragedy. He was widely read in schools and universities; his thoughts, extracted from treatises as well as plays, were recorded in commonplace books; his plays were dutifully translated. (In 1581 Seneca's ten tragedies had all been translated and published in one volume; by 1561, when *Gorboduc* was acted, four of the plays had been translated.)

Seneca appealed to the Elizabethan mind because of the political nature of his thought, because his heroes pointed to the individualism of the Renaissance supermen, and because his stoical stance fitted in well with current Elizabethan thinking. In addition, the Elizabethans found in Seneca an ornate and elevated style, a rhetoric, which they were educated to love. Sidney's praise of *Gorboduc* — that it climbs the height of Seneca's style — indicates the respect of the learned for Seneca. Contemporary evidence of this admiration is so pervasive that it is difficult not to consider Seneca an important influence on Renaissance thought and Renaissance drama.

However, Seneca's undeniable influence on Elizabethan drama in general has led some critics to present exaggerated views about his specific importance to *Gorboduc* — a view which has led other critics to reject Seneca almost completely. H. Schmidt,[22] in 1887, was the first scholar to attribute the Classical influence on *Gorboduc* to Seneca alone. Six years later the influential study by John W. Cunliffe,[23] which presented a comprehensive and detailed study of the debt of *Gorboduc* to Seneca, gave Seneca the credit of providing not only the external form of the play (division into five acts separated by choruses), but also specific speeches, aphorisms, and kernels of thought. Cunliffe presents parallel after parellel to suggest the reliance of Sackville and Norton on Seneca's moralizings about fate, fortune, death, the impetuosity of youth, and the pitfalls of pride. He presents quotation after quotation to indicate the use of Seneca's mythological allusions and descriptions. Cunliffe's lead was followed by Felix E. Schelling,[24] F. L. Lucas,[25] and T. S. Eliot,[26] all devoting their attention to Senecan influence. Homer Watt's study, although acknowledging influences other than Seneca, agrees substantially with Cunliffe. By quoting and by specifying parallels, he indicates that *Gorboduc* is "saturated with Senecan influence," and that it imitates Seneca in form, style, and phraseology. He agrees with Schmidt's contention that "the classical influence is due only to Seneca."[27]

These views have been opposed vigorously by Howard Baker,[28] who refuses to label *Gorboduc* a "Senecan" play. He states that the mode of division into five acts was taken in all likelihood from Classical comedy. He considers the chorus a logical descendant of the commentator in such metrical tragedies as are found in *The Mirror for Magistrates,* and he traces the messenger back to the Medieval mystery and morality plays. He asserts that Sackville and Norton could have found "Senecan" diction and "Senecan" sententiousness in sources other than Seneca, like the Bible. And he insists that "the real morality in *Gorboduc* is the reverse of Senecan morality."[29] In short, Baker attempts to refute the supporters of

Seneca by using their evidence to suggest other sources. He considerably minimizes, almost erases, the influence of the Latin dramatist.

Willard Farnham leans heavily toward Baker's view that *Gorboduc,* like most Elizabethan tragedy, does not evolve from Senecan tragedy. He does call the play "Senecan" because of the formality of its scenes, but he attaches the play to the popular native tragic tradition rather than to the learned Classical tradition.[30]

The Senecan influence on *Gorboduc,* therefore, called forth opposing views based on much of the same evidence. Part of the problem stems from difficulties attached to every "source" or "influence" study, difficulties which I have discussed in Chapter 3. In an age when imitation was regarded as the duty of the writer and in a work that displays a Renaissance synthesis (and is therefore complex by necessity), it is often difficult to isolate an influence with a great degree of assurance. Indeed, part of the problem is caused by the attitude of the scholar; for moderation and the willingness to acknowledge a margin for doubt must be part of the scholar's stance when he searches for influences. Because of this lack, both Cunliffe and Baker, although they present valuable studies of *Gorboduc,* seem to skirt the truth which is located somewhere between the enthusiasms of their opposing views. The most intelligent discussions of Senecan influence have come from those writers who tread more cautiously — namely, Marvin T. Herrick,[31] Henry W. Wells,[32] and Paul Bacquet.[33]

Herrick, who grants Baker his arguments without denying the importance of Senecan influence, states that the five-act structure probably stems from the plays of Terence, but he admits Seneca's tragedies were divided into five acts and were well known in England. He believes that Sackville and Norton could have found the moralizing choruses at the end of each act in other places but that they probably found the device in Seneca's tragedies. He emphasizes that Seneca does use a messenger and that he does present rant and *sententiae.* In short, Herrick reviews the usual "Senecan" aspects of the play to suggest that it is probable that Sackville and Norton derive them from Seneca but that the play is not "merely Senecan." He tests the Senecan parallels presented by his predecessors and identifies influences other than Seneca and, in addition, finds Senecan parallels in thought not noticed by Cunliffe and company — discussing such general ideas as the fickleness of fortune and the "aura of political morality which surrounds the work." He presents the best approach to the problem because he acknowledges and proves that "the predominant classical influence in *Gorboduc* is Senecan" at the same time that he recognizes the complexity of the work and sees it as a synthesis of the Classical, Medieval, and contemporary.

The limitations of the views represented by Cunliffe and Baker are also recognized by Henry W. Wells, who insists that no one has looked closely at Seneca. The term "Senecan" is not helpful and is essentially uncritical, he maintains, because the ten tragedies of Seneca differ widely from one another. He, like Baker, finds the usual Senecan characteristics to be superficial and not necessarily Senecan. Wells believes that we have associated Seneca's influence with the wrong things, such as stylistic mannerisms and the use of physical horror. He sees Seneca's appeal to the Elizabethans as stemming from "his real poetic merits, his mirror of an age of material progress and spiritual decay, his increased emphasis upon political or public degeneration, and on the role of the individual."[34] These qualities are found more in late tragedy than in *Gorboduc,* but they point to a sensible approach to Senecan influence.

Bacquet, who approaches the problem with characteristic prudence and thoroughness, refuses to consider *Gorboduc* as a purely Senecan piece, although he acknowledges and examines those aspects of the play which seem Senecan to him — the atmosphere, some of the themes, the dramatic structure, the characterization of Videna, the language and style. He presents the most detailed examination of the problem but cautiously avoids the exaggerations of his predecessors. Most important, he is ever aware of the complexity of the work as a product of a Renaissance synthesis.

That *Gorboduc* is an important example of Senecan tragedy is a commonplace of literary history. Like most commonplaces, it needs examination — but examination of "influence" really means pointed discussion within a *range* of possibility. It is reasonable, I think, to state the following about Senecan influence on *Gorboduc.* Sackville and Norton were familiar with Seneca's plays — in the original Latin and in those translations made before 1561. They were educated to appreciate the kind of rhetoric associated with Seneca; and, as statesmen, they would be receptive to the political nature of his thought. They probably derived from Seneca the formal aspects of the play — division into five acts, subdivided into scenes; the chorus at the end of four acts; violent action taking place off-stage; use of the messenger to report off-stage action; and no strict adherence to the Classical unities.

But even such a guarded statement needs qualification: the five-act structure may have come from Classical comedy; the chorus in *Gorboduc* is more detached than in Seneca and it explains the non-Senecan dumb show preceding each act; one messenger in *Gorboduc,* Marcella, takes on an importance not given to Senecan messengers; the absence of unities — to the chagrin of Sidney — could stem directly from the dramatists' political purpose rather than from any influence on a Classical playwright. (A Senecan characteristic which does not appear in *Gorboduc* is the ghost — not, as Watt believes, because a ghost might detract from the play's seriousness, but rather because a ghost, suggesting an evil past and a curse, does not fit neatly into a tragedy caused by the mistake of a good king.)

The long, high-sounding, dignified, rhetorical speeches in *Gorboduc* are in the Senecan manner, as are the grave precepts and certain aspects of diction: the use of the descriptive adjective; the use of "hand" and "heart," corresponding to Seneca's *manus* and *animus;* the allusions to famous names in ancient history. Even here other influences may have played a part — the long speeches in the Medieval plays, the sententiousness of parts of the Bible, the diction of the Psalms — but Sackville and Norton probably derived many aspects of language and style from the Latin dramatist.

Atmosphere is a difficult quality to attribute to an influence, but the gravity of *Gorboduc,* unrelieved by any hint of the comic, seems Senecan. The miracle and morality plays often blended the tragic and comic, whereas the plays in the Classical tradition present horror and blood and gloom without relief. Again, Sackville and Norton may have been influenced more by their own serious purpose than by their reliance on Seneca, but the somber atmosphere, reinforced by the frequent allusion to a mythological past, inevitably reminds us of Seneca.

Even more difficult to assess, and requiring the most prudent approach, are the themes that we find in *Gorboduc;* for often, as indicated in my discussion of the "Induction," we are dealing with commonplaces of thought. The theme of the fickleness of fortune is Senecan; but it could be derived directly from that Christian Seneca, Boethius. The theme of "blood will have blood" is as Hebraic as it is Senecan. The idea of impetuosity of youth is a cultural commonplace, which could be derived from Cicero as well as Seneca. The political themes — obedience to one ruler, fickleness of the mob, etc. — are found in the Bible, in Tudor chronicles, in Classical writers other than Seneca, although Seneca does dwell on these themes and was important in the Elizabethan age partly because of the political nature of his thought. In discussing themes, therefore, Seneca's name may be used but only in connection with other influences. At the very least, however, Seneca, part of the acquired equipment of every educated Elizabethan, reinforced the thinking of Sackville and Norton on the important themes found in *Gorboduc.*

One theme, that of revenge, deserves closer attention at this point. The spirit of vengeance is integral to many of Seneca's plays and may have had an important effect on two aspects of *Gorboduc* — one, in connection with character; the other and more significant, in connection with structure and having implications that go beyond *Gorboduc.* The only character in *Gorboduc* who is truly Senecan is Videna.[35] She, like most of Seneca's characters, is not so much a physical presence, a flesh and blood character, as an emotional presence. The aura of vengeance and death surrounds her, and she calls to mind the Furies. Her crime, killing her kin, allies her to Medea; her motive, like Medea's, is vengeance. She strikes the note of revenge in the play's first scene — here a "just revenge" as she calls it — and she typifies revenge in the passion of her rhetorical (Senecan?) speech which constitutes Act IV, Scene 1. The decisiveness, even rigidity, and the blood and horror that we associate with Senecan characters cling to Videna, a Senecan creature.

Revenge is also important to the play's structure. It allows for a chain of cause and effect, of act and counteract, which gives the play direction and a sense of unity. Porrex kills Ferrex, Videna kills Porrex, the people kill Gorboduc and Videna, the nobles kill the leaders of the people. The deaths are consequential; the play has a shape. A quick look at the structure of *Cambises,* a play that is not Senecan, indicates how important the revenge motif can be to a play. In *Cambises* deaths occur in mechanical fashion, with the tyrant Cambises killing various people and then getting killed himself by accident. No action provokes a counteraction; no motive informs the deaths. The play is loose, episodic, directionless. In *Gorboduc* the motive of revenge, which Sackville and Norton saw *in use* in Senecan drama, shapes the course of action and allows the dramatists to present a play that is satisfyingly patterned. The large structural effect stemming from Seneca's use of revenge is surely a more important contribution to the development of Elizabethan drama than the more often quoted characteristics of Senecan dramaturgy (five-act structure, chorus, etc.). Senecan tragedy probably gave the theme of revenge its impetus on the Elizabethan stage, and it thereby had a lasting effect on the structure of Elizabethan tragedy.[36]

The question of Senecan influence on *Gorboduc* in particular and on Elizabethan drama in general will continue to attract discussion. Senecan influence cannot be denied, but a prudent examination of possible "Senecan" characteristics is more fruitful, I believe, than a partisan discussion upholding a specific label or an equally partisan discussion attacking that label.

VI *Native Influences*

Gorboduc also owes a clear debt to native influences; Sackville and Norton, in true Renaissance fashion, chose what they wished from all that was available to them, native as well as Classical; and they managed to blend gracefully aspects of both the Classical and native traditions. *Gorboduc* belongs to the didactic tradition of the morality plays, in which lessons were taught and debates were held between the forces of good and evil. The typical morality play had a basic plot scheme in which Man or Mankind or Everyman is torn between good and evil, succumbs to evil, sins (usually in a tavern world where he can be gluttonous and lecherous), realizes his mistake, becomes converted to good, and is thereby saved from eternal damnation.[37] At stake in the morality play is Man's soul, so that the struggle is a religious one.

Sackville and Norton, in morality fashion, balance the forces of good and evil surrounding Gorboduc and his sons — so that Gorboduc must choose between the advice of the good Eubulus and the less good Arostus ("evil" is too strong a word for him); Ferrex, between the advice of the good Dordan and the evil Hermon; and Porrex, between the good Philander and the evil Tyndor. However, in *Gorboduc* the advice concerns not the status of man's soul but the welfare of England. (In this respect, the play resembles the morality play, *Respublica* [1553], which also is concerned with politics and is "contemporary.") The moral is political. Gorboduc and his sons, following bad advice, cause chaos in the commonwealth. No conversion takes place in the individual or restoration in the state (at least during the play's action). The dramatists adopt part of the morality scheme to suit their didactic purpose. They also allow their good and bad counselors to approach abstractions, again in morality fashion. Although the counselors have the names of men (and therefore are not, strictly speaking, personifications, like Good Council or Bad Living), they possess no identity apart from the advice they give; they are merely mouthpieces for a point of view. They, like most characters in *Gorboduc* and in morality plays, do not psychologize. Some have names that carry morality-like meanings: Eubulus means Good Will; Philander is a Loving Man.

The didactic nature of *Gorboduc* suggests another native influence — the "tragical narrative" tradition, which includes Lydgate and *The Mirror for Magistrates.* It is not surprising that Thomas Sackville, an important contributor to the *Mirror,* should use his play as a "mirror" which will allow Queen Elizabeth to see the career of Gorboduc as a warning to her. That the past must teach the present is the didactic base of the *Mirror* narratives and of the very chronicles to which Sackville and Norton went for the sources of *Gorboduc.* To teach their lesson, the dramatists did not go to the mythology of Seneca but to the history of their own land, indicating an obvious, but potent, aspect of native influence.

Gorboduc contains specific passages which seem to come directly from Chaucer, the Psalms, and the Bible. Bacquet sees Chaucer's *Complaynte unto Pitie* as a possible source for Marcella's pathetic monologue.[38] Baker finds the play's "Senecan vocabulary" in the very psalms that Norton translated.[39] Watt examines some Biblical echoes in the play.[40] But the most dynamic and important native element in *Gorboduc* is the dumb show, which also is directly related to the didactic purpose of the play. For the first time in English drama we have acts introduced by pantomimic scenes, silent prologues which are explained verbally by the chorus at the ends of the acts.

Each dumb show illustrates the moral of the act and is therefore connected with the didactic thrust of the play, but the characters in the dumb shows are not the characters in the play itself. They are symbolic or allegorical. In addition, the dumb shows provide a visual spectacle which is lacking in the body of the play. Of the five dumb shows, two, the third and fifth, are primarily atmospheric. In the third, mourners clad in black pass about the stage three times; and, in the fifth, soldiers discharge pieces and march about the stage to the accompaniment of drums and flutes. The first and second dumb shows are complete scenes which have a direct thematic bearing on the play. The first, based on a fable, presents six wild men who attempt to break a fagot of small sticks, fail, but then break the sticks individually. The second contains the spectacle of two men giving the king drink — one offers wine in a glass, the other offers poison in a cup of gold. The king chooses the latter and dies. The fourth dumb show, lively and colorful, is symbolic: the three Furies appear on stage, bloody and girt with snakes, driving before them unnatural kings and queens. Each of the dumb shows is vitally connected with the act which it precedes, and all contribute to the play's total effect.

Not all commentators believe that the dumb show is a native contribution. Cunliffe argues that the dumb shows are influenced by the Italian *intermedii,* placed between the acts of Italian neo-classical plays.[41] They probably were seen by Englishmen visiting Italy and known even to those Englishmen who remained home. These *intermedii* were allegorical, usually accompanied by music; some contained speaking and singing parts; some presented pantomime only. They became very popular, perhaps more popular than the comedies into which they were thrust. But these between-act performances lack some of the important features of the dumb show in *Gorboduc.* They appear at the end of the act, not at the beginning; they are usually associated with comedy, not tragedy; they have little relationship to the play itself.

It is not necessary to look beyond the shores of England to find prototypes for the dumb show. Medieval drama often contained pageantry; the Corpus Christi processions were part of the Medieval scene; allegorical processions were witnessed on special holidays. (Elizabeth's coronation procession, we can assume, was seen by Sackville, kin to the queen.) However, the most obvious forerunner of the dumb show in *Gorboduc* seems to be the London street pageants,[42] which displayed pictorial representations symbolizing political or historical events, which contained actors who personified allegorical figures, and which presented an explanation of the allegory either by scroll or actor. Court masques may also have had their influence, since they contained music, a pantomimic action, spectacle, and symbolic representations.

In short, the obvious prototypes of the dumb show were displayed and witnessed by the dramatists in their own land. It was left for them to use aspects of these prototypes imaginatively and to incorporate them in what was ostensibly a new dramatic device. The dumb shows not only have an important function in *Gorboduc,* as my later commentary indicates, but paved the way for incorporation of dumb shows in later Elizabethan drama.

VII *Blank Verse*

That *Gorboduc* was the first English play written in blank verse is so important an historical fact that it has guaranteed *Gorboduc's* place in every English literary history. T. S. Eliot could claim with assurance and justification that *Gorboduc* "makes a new epoch; there is no clearer division in the whole of English literature."[43] How Sackville and Norton came to use blank verse as their measure — thereby changing the course of Elizabethan drama — must remain a debatable question.

The earliest English blank verse was written by Henry Howard, Earl of Surrey, in his translation of the second and fourth books of Virgil's *Aeniad,* published in 1557. Surrey probably attempted to reproduce in English the quantitative Latin verse, although his syllable-counting technique seems contrary to the principles of Classical prosody. It is too easy to say with Howard Baker that "Surrey simply wrote his decasyllables without rhyme,"[44] for this view tends to minimize the persistent effort on the part of English poets to force English verse into the quantitative mold. Perhaps Surrey was encouraged by the tradition of Middle English unrhymed alliterative verse. (Surely he was aware of the dislike for rhyme by such Classicists as Roger Ascham and Sir John Cheke.) Perhaps Surrey was influenced by the Italian *versi sciolti* found in Cardinal Ippolito de Medici's translation of the second book of the *Aeniad* and in Trissino's epic, *Italia liberatat dai Goti,* and his drama, *Sophinisba;* but, whatever prompted Surrey, his use of blank verse in the translation of an epic marked an important event in English literature.

Nicholas Grimald, lecturer on rhetoric at Christchurch, Oxford, wrote two short narrative poems in blank verse — *Marcius Tullius Cicero's Death* and *The Death of Zoroas* — which were both contributed to *Tottel's Miscellany* (1557). At about this time, Queen Elizabeth translated into blank verse passages from the second act of *Hercules Oetaeus,* one of Seneca's tragedies.

Of special interest to a discussion of *Gorboduc* is the use of blank verse by one of its authors, Thomas Norton, in his translation of Calvin's *Institutes of the Christian Religion.* Calvin quotes a passage from Virgil's *Aeniad,* Book VI, and a passage from Virgil's

Georgics, Book IV. Norton, obviously following Surrey's example, renders these quotations into blank verse — thereby providing a specific and positive link between the blank verse of Surrey and the blank verse of *Gorboduc.*[45]

It is indisputable, therefore, that Sackville and Norton were both familiar with blank verse and that the use of the measure was part of a general humanistic impulse in Italy and England. (Classical literature was taught by Cheke at Cambridge and by Grimald at Oxford.) The transition of blank verse from a predominantly epic to a dramatic meter may have been effected by Queen Elizabeth's use in her Senecan translation, of which her kinsman Sackville must have been cognizant. Sackville and Norton may have seen the meter as an adaptation in English of the tragic meter and style of Seneca. We should always remind ourselves that for Sidney *Gorboduc* did climb to the height "of Seneca his style." Perhaps either Sackville or Norton, by an act of creative imagination, realized that the newly created measure, usually used for epic purposes, had great dramatic potential. Whatever the suggesting influence, the fact that Sackville and Norton used blank verse in a play for the first time is of high importance.

Although *Gorboduc* is always given credit for introducing blank verse to English drama — a fact of literary history — it is usually condemned for the blank verse it uses, a fact of literary criticism. Most critics see little resemblance between the blank verse of *Gorboduc* and that of Marlowe and Shakespeare. They criticize the verse for its "stiffness and dead uniformity,"[46] its "inflexible regularity" which is "wearisomely pedantic and long-winded,"[47] its "wooden blankness,"[48] and so on. There is so remarkable a continuity in these charges against the versification of *Gorboduc,* the view is so widespread, that we are tempted merely to restate the condemnation and move on. But pause we must, because the charges against the mechanics of the verse are not supported by close examination.

S. F. Johnson, in his unpublished doctoral dissertation, has refuted convincingly the usual explanations for the play's woodenness. He demonstrates that there is variation in the verse, that *Gorboduc* has many run-on lines (about the same proportion as *Hamlet*) and feminine endings, that end-stopping is not necessarily the rule. In short, the metrical pattern is not so rigidly conceived as critics have stated; and the play's monotony has little to do with the mechanics of the blank verse.[49] Johnson points to origins for the monotony that are more conceptual than metrical, and in doing so he correctly places *Gorboduc* in the rhetorical tradition which is so important a part of Sackville's art. The impression of "dead uniformity," etc., arises from the rhetorical structure of the play.

The blank verse of *Gorboduc* does not suggest the flexibility of Shakespeare's later plays because it is subject to the ends of rhetoric. The formality of the pattern in *Gorboduc* is deliberate — pointing not to the poetic deficiencies of its authors but to the needs they wish to serve. Sackville and Norton *deliberately* repeat words, manipulate similar sounds, build lines on alliterative doublets, balance adjective and noun against adjective and noun in the same line. The rhetorical balance of their blank-verse line is not far removed from many of Marlowe's important lines.[50] With time, of course, the strict formality of the line decreased, but in the best hands a degree of formality combined with sufficient flexibility to produce dramatic dialogue of the highest order.[51] If *Gorboduc* is on one end of the scale, displaying blank verse of such formality that it can be considered dull and wooden, then Fletcher is on the other end of the scale, since his verse is so loose that for many it may not qualify as verse at all. Between these extremes, we find the best of Elizabethan poetic drama.

The blank verse of *Gorboduc* often annoys our ears, which, after all, have heard Shakespeare. It is precisely because of this reaction that we should stress not only the important fact that Sackville and Norton were the first to use a verse medium that would take Elizabethan drama to its highest achievement, but that the verse itself admirably suits the specific rhetorical purposes of the dramatists.

VIII *Commentary*

"The Argument of the Tragedie" leads us to expect *Gorboduc* to be filled with incident and movement:

> Gorboduc, king of Brittaine, diuided his realme in his lifetime to his sonnes, Ferrex and Porrex; the sonnes fell to discention; the yonger killed the elder; the mother, that more dearely loued the elder, for reuenge killed the yonger; the people, moued with the crueltie of the fact, rose in rebellion and slew both father and mother; the nobilities assembled and most terribly destroyed the rebels; and afterwardes, for want of issue of the prince, whereby the succession of the crowne became vncertaine, they fell to ciuill warre, in which both they and many of their issues were slaine, and the land for a long time almost desolate and miserably wasted.

But such expectation is not fulfilled. All of the important "action" scenes take place off stage. We *hear* about them; and speech, therefore, gives the play its essential life. Because *Gorboduc* is didactic, political, and argumentative, because what happens does not seem to be as important as the moral implications of what happens, the play gives the basic impression of people *talking*. This talk, this apparently static quality of the play, has won the displeasure of most modern students of the drama. But speech can be an effective dramatic instrument, and emphasis on rhetoric need not preclude theatrical effectiveness, especially speech that presents both intellectual debate *and* emotional outpouring; cold deliberation *and* passionate feeling — all stemming from conflict, the essence of drama. And, when the "speech" scenes are introduced by active dumb shows, what is heard is being anticipated by what is seen.

The play begins with noise and spectacle when six wild men clothed in leaves appear on stage to the sounds of violins. They attempt to break a fagot of small sticks, cannot, but then each plucks out a stick and breaks it. After all the sticks are broken, the men leave, and the music ceases. The printed version of the play explains the obvious significance of the action immediately after describing the dumb show; the chorus, four ancient and sage men, explains the action at the end of the first act. The dumb show is vitally connected to the act which it precedes, for in Act I, Scene 2 a king will divide his country, which will be destroyed easily because of his division. But this first dumb show is related to more than the plot of the first act; it foreshadows the chaos of the entire play; "wilde men" are the forces of disorder always present in a state, ready to be unleashed when the natural order of things is upset.

The noise and the wildness of the dumb show also provide an effective contrast to Videna's quiet opening words and a reinforcement of the torment in her heart:

> The silent night, that bringes the quiet pawse
> From painefull trauailes of the wearie day,
> Prolonges my carefull thoughtes, and makes me blame
> The slowe Aurore, that so for loue or shame
> Doth long delay to shewe her blushing face;
> And now the day renewes my griefull plaint.
> (I,1,1-6)

The references to nature set the tone and remind us of the opening lines of the "Induction." Videna is talking to her eldest and favorite son, Ferrex; and their dialogue reveals the tender love they feel for each other, allowing us to understand Videna's present anxiety for her son and her later action against Porrex. What perturbs her is Gorboduc's plan to divide the land between the brothers; she wishes all of it for Ferrex, who, as the older son, should become king of the whole kingdom. Her words characterize her as a revengeful woman who intensely dislikes her younger son — whom she describes as proud, envious, and ambitious — and who has contempt for her husband, who is acting "against all lawe and right." Ferrex reinforces her image of the proud Porrex, but he denies the unjust intentions of his father, who has always been a good man. He hopes for the best, but Videna presents words filled with foreboding:

> When lordes, and trusted rulers vnder kinges,
> To please the present fancie of the prince,
> With wrong transpose the course of gouernance,
> Murders, mischiefe, or ciuill sword at length,
> Or mutuall treason, or a iust reuenge
> When right-succeding line returnes againe,
> By Ioues iust iudgement and deserued wrath
> Bringes them to cruell and reprochfull death,
> And rootes their names and kindredes from the earth.
> (I,1,59-67)

The important elements of the play are here — evil advisers, revenge, chaos, God's judgment. The speech immediately precedes the ominous word-play which ends the scene:

FERREX: Mother, content you; you shall see the end.
VIDENA: The end? Thy end, I feare! Iove end me first!

This opening scene, short as it is (sixty-nine lines), presents a praiseworthy combination of exposition and characterization and foreshadowing. It reveals important facts of plot, which are repeated in the next scene, indicates relationship of character, and offers value judgments of characters yet to appear. And it alludes to the motifs that bind the play together.

This darkly foreboding scene is followed by one that is abstract, argumentative, and obviously didactic. Gorboduc gets the advice of his three lords about the proposed division of the realm, but the advice seems to exist for its own sake, since his mind cannot be changed — "In one self purpose do I still abide." His genuine love of country, "mother of us all," and his love for order confirm his position as a good king; but his foolish decision will lead to the chaos he fears.

Most of the scene consists of the three long speeches by his advisers. Arostus, always ready to give easy advice, fully approves of the king's plan. Philander would modify the plan by having it come into effect when the king dies, so that Gorboduc's present behavior as king could be a lesson for his sons. Eubulus, the mouthpiece for the dramatists throughout the play, argues against the plan:

> Within one land one single rule is best:
> Diuided reignes do make diuided hartes:
> But peace preserues the countrey and the prince.
> Suche is in man the gredy minde to reigne,
> So great is his desire to climbe alofte,
> In worldly stage the stateliest partes to beare,
> That faith and iustice and all kindly loue
> Do yelde vnto desire of soueraignitie
> Where egall state doth raise an egall hope
> To winne the thing that either wold attaine.
> (I,2,259-68)

Here Eubulus succinctly expresses the Tudor ideal of unity and indicates what must happen when that unity is broken. More than this, however, he presents an attitude toward the nature of man that must be reckoned with throughout the play: man is *by nature* greedy and ambitious; he must be kept in check by sovereignty, or chaos will come. In fact, chaos will come *again,* for Eubulus later presents history as proof that division creates disorder. His reference to the Brute story is important; for, just as Eubulus goes to historical example to support a political argument, so Sackville and Norton go to the very history of Gorboduc's reign to emphasize their political intent. History should teach; but, alas, Eubulus' advice is not taken. Gorboduc will divide Britain, but as a precaution he will give his sons good advisers. Since he did not listen to the good advice offered him, the gesture does not seem a workable antidote to a foolish judgment. The chorus, which ends the act by verbalizing the fable presented in the dumb show, alludes to Phaethon, that proud son of Apollo who rashly "inflamed the parched earth with heavens fire," and emphasizes the folly of the King's decision in the last stanza:

> And this great king, that doth deuide his land,
> And chaunge the course of his discending crowne,

> And yeldes the reigne into his childrens hande,
> From blisfull state of ioye and great renowne
> A myrrour shall become to princes all
> To learn to shunne the cause of suche a fall.
> (I,2,19-24)

The words are charged with significance. The "myrrour" places Gorboduc in the didactic "fall of princes" tradition; here is one more example from history that should teach. The mirror should be for princes to look into, that is, for magistrates — including Queen Elizabeth. The "fall" of the very last line not only indicates the fall of princes, but surely harks back to the Phaethon image — the fall of pride, of rebellious youth, thereby pointing ahead to Porrex as well. And the "fall" signifies the falling action of the play, for everything goes *down* after Gorboduc's decision to divide the land. The kingdom was comparatively healthy for one act only; the rest is chaos.

This wordy scene, weighing an argument from different points of view, formal, almost ceremonious, ends with a heavy word, "fall," which points to a tradition and recalls a mythical figure, Phaethon. The word is followed by the music of cornets that begins the second dumb show; the action of the dumb show is again directly related to the plot of the act it precedes; for a king, choosing a golden cup filled with poison offered by a young courtier rather than a clear glass filled with wine offered by a grave and aged gentleman, immediately drops dead on stage.

The obvious balancing of the good and evil advisers in the dumb show is exactly duplicated in the two scenes of Act II, and the didactic morality tradition appears behind dumb show and scenes. In the first scene, Ferrex wonders why he has been robbed of half his kingdom, which was his "of law and nature." The parasite Hermon suggests that he kill his brother and seize the entire kingdom; but Ferrex, always a good man, will not put "such mischiefe" in his heart. Instead, he will secretly arm against a possible attack by his brother, who is again characterized as proud, envious, and full of hate. This scene carries on the "advice" motif, confirms our attitudes about both Ferrex and Porrex, contains many references to law and nature, and alludes again both to Brute and Phaethon in order that history and mythology should teach. The scene presents one puzzling note when Dordan, the good counselor, rejects Ferrex's characterization of his brother. Dordan never witnessed Porrex's pride, he says, and finds Porrex to be wise and "of noble hope." Either Sackville and Norton are suggesting that even a good adviser can be mistaken or they wish us to be uncertain about Porrex's true character. This ambivalence concerning Porrex is displayed later in the play and indicates a complexity of character often found in the more mature Elizabethan drama.

Porrex's evil adviser Tyndar is more successful with his envious prince. Reporting to Porrex about Ferrex's secret preparations, he stirs Porrex to express his ambition and treachery. Porrex's own words seem to indicate the truth of the evaluations of his character given by Videna and Ferrex, and set him up as an obvious foil to Ferrex. Philander, before rushing off to inform Gorboduc of Porrex's state of mind, bemoans the condition of the commonwealth and alludes to the fall of Troy and the avenging gods. The Chorus, explaining the significance of the second dumb show, also alludes to the angry gods and effectively suggests the immediacy of the impending chaos with such words as "swelling," "climbing," and "growing." Immediate it is, for at this moment the mourners of the third dumb show, all clad in black, pass about the stage to the music of flutes; and the atmosphere of death pervades the rest of the play.

Act III, the central act, is the most static one in the play; for in it Gorboduc receives various pieces of news stemming from his initial act of dividing the kingdom. Here, more than in any other act, we feel that the real play is being acted on some other stage. Information about Ferrex's defensive preparations is contained in a letter from Dordan. Information about Porrex's intended treachery is presented in person by Philander. And then, before the information can be acted upon, a messenger reports that Porrex has killed Ferrex "with his owne most bloudy hand." A scene containing merely a presentation of news can hardly be considered effective drama, but the tone saves the scene from dullness. The dramatists play heavily on the ironies that result from the news that comes in piecemeal.

Gorboduc, having read the letter from Dordan offstage, shouts out against the "still-continued rage" of the gods against the Britons, descendants of the Trojans. We can never forget that we are dealing with history. If there must be revenge, he hopes the gods will make him and his sons their victims, not "this giltlesse realme" — which again emphasizes the basic goodness of Gorboduc. He says he has gathered his counselors "to have your good advyse." Surely we must think back to the last time he gathered them in order *not* to take good advice. The statement, and our remembrance of things past, immediately undercuts whatever advice the scene will contain. After Dordan's letter is read aloud, Arostus, the master of easy advice, assures Gorboduc that all will be well, that "timely knowledge may bring timely helpe." At this moment Philander enters. Gorboduc's salute, "The goddes sende joyfull newes!" is answered by Philander's ominous report of Porrex's preparation for war, including one more account of Porrex's wrath and ambition. Gorboduc again refers to the curse on his house — "Iove slay them [both sons] and end the cursed line!" It is now Philander's turn to soothe Gorboduc:

> Yelde not, O king, so much to weake dispeire!
> Your sonnes yet lyue, and long, I trust they shall.
> . . . .
> That louyng Ioue hath tempred so the time
> Of this debate to happen in your dayes
> That you yet lyuing may the same appeaze
> And adde it to the glory of your latter age,
> And they, your sonnes, may learne to liue in peace.
> (III,1,104-5,119-23)

The messenger of Ferrex's death rushes on stage to burst the bubble of optimism. Gorboduc's reaction to the news (and the last words of the scene before the choric utterance) is:

> O Heauens, send down the flames of your reuenge!
> Destroy, I say, with flash of wrekefull fier
> The traitour sonne, and then the wretched sire!
> But let vs go, that yet perhappes I may
> Die with reuenge, and peaze the hatefull gods.
> (III,1,163-67)

The words bring back the realistic perspective. The advice was too easy, an initial act of bad judgment has unleashed unnatural and inevitable forces, the "loving Jove" has become "the hateful gods." The obvious, almost mechanical, juxtapositions of soothing advice followed by bad news, high hopes followed by utter dejection, loving gods followed by hateful gods make the ironies of the scene so heavy that we are tempted to believe that Sackville and Norton are appealing directly to the intelligent, sophisticated, and probably cynical students of the Inns of Court. The audience does not need the Chorus to tell of heaven's wrath, of vengeance, of the "giltie race," and of the "dead black streames of mourning" that flow from civil war.

How effective must have been the entrance of the Furies at this point. After straight information and heavy irony, spectacle is a relief. This spectacle is both relief and highly symbolic — a visual and musical presentation of unnatural murder and supernatural retribution. The high-pitched oboes pierce the air as Alecto, Megaera, and Tisiphone, three Furies loosed out of Hell (under the stage) — snaky-haired; black garments sprinkled with blood and flames — drive before them six kings and queens who had slain their own children. We must assume that the audience knew the identities of the figures named in the printed edition: Tantalus, Medea, Athamas, Ino, Cambises, Althea. The procession of guilty royalty is reminiscent of a similar ghostly procession in *The Mirror for Magistrates*.

The dumb show has a direct relationship to the fourth act of the play in which other unnatural murders will occur — a mother will kill a son; a rebellious people will kill a king and queen. Just as the dramatists used Classical allusions in the speeches to indicate a continuity in history and to give added significance to the happenings in the play, so they present a mythological pantomime to give the same effect. But now the effect is atmospheric. The hideousness of the crimes can be *seen;* the unnaturalness can be punctuated by the discordant music. The audience is forced to experience on another level of sensibility the unnatural effects of unnatural crime.

Videna, who enters now, is surrounded by an aura of vengeance and death. Her eighty-one line soliloquy fills the entire scene. The words are so forceful, so emotional, that we are forced to believe that they were written by a new writer. (As noted previously, external evidence points to Sackville as the writer of Acts IV and V; most scholars consider Videna Sackville's creation.) Here the play's didacticism and politics give way to emotion as Videna laments the loss of her favorite son and vows revenge on her younger son. She wishes for her own death, the peace of death where the pain of "greadie wormes" gnawing her suffering heart would not be felt. Her apostrophe to Ferrex allows us to feel her terrible loss and helps in part to soften her later act of villainy:

> O my beloued sonne! O my swete childe!
> My deare Ferrex, my ioye, my lyues delyght!
> Is my beloued sonne, is my sweete childe,

> My deare Ferrex, my ioye, my lyues delight,
> Murdered with cruell death?
> (IV, 1, 23-26)

Her words on Porrex display seething hatred:

> O hatefull wretch!
> O heynous traitour both to heauen and earth!
> Thou, Porrex, thou this damned dede hast wrought!
> Thou, Porrex, thou shalt dearely bye the same!
> Traitour to kinne and kinde, to sire and me,
> To thine owne fleshe, and traitour to thyselfe,
> The gods on thee in hell shall wreke their wrath,
> And here in earth this hand shall take reuenge
> On thee, Porrex, thou false and caitife wight!
> (IV, 1, 26-35)

Videna's anger seems uncontrollable as she lashes out against Porrex with curses that make us think of Shakespeare's Margaret in *Richard III.* She wrings pathos as she refers to her womb from which came both the murderous Porrex and the "sweete life" of Ferrex. That she is a *mother* is stressed again and again:

> Ruthelesse, vnkinde, monster of natures worke,
> Thou neuer suckt the milke of womans brest,
> But from thy birth the cruell tigers teates
> Haue nursed thee!
> (IV, 1, 71-74)

The soliloquy — high-pitched, grievous, pathetic, furious — is given a Shakespearean specificity by means of references to worms, graves, wombs, teats, and milk; and it is no small dramatic feat. True, as Clemen indicates,[52] its antitheses and parallels are grouped, it is systematic and organized — pleasing, no doubt, to the legalistic Inns of Court audience — but the passion breaks through the rhetorical strictures to reveal an emotional presence, a malignity that is not motiveless, a creature of dark revenge, which she calls "just revenge." Videna's soliloquy, coupled with the preceding dumb show, allows us to experience vividly the impending tragedy.

This one-character, intense scene is followed by the play's most crowded scene, one in which Porrex is brought to judgment before Gorboduc for his devastating deed and in which the murder of

Porrex is reported. The Gorboduc-Porrex confrontation contains in part the built-in conflict of most trial scenes in drama, but only in part; for the speeches are relatively calm, and the confrontation seems mechanical. Gorboduc's speech of accusation contains many references to blood and revenge, but his main thrust is that Porrex's deed offended the law of nature and therefore "Natures force doth move us to revenge/ By bloud againe, and justice forceth us/ To measure death for death." When Porrex answers the accusation with two speeches, one expresses remorse without asking for pardon; the other relates the events which led to the murder. Porrex's defense of himself is somewhat puzzling. His words suggest that he is genuine in his remorse — although an actor's gesture and tone could betray his true feelings. His ostensible softness here jars against the impression we had of him up to now, except for Dordan's words about his nobility. Porrex characterizes Ferrex with the very qualities we have attached to Porrex — envy, deceit, treachery — which leads us to believe that Sackville is allowing him to characterize himself, an interesting and sophisticated use of dramatic irony. Still, it *could* be that Porrex is genuinely repentant, which gives the account of his death an added poignancy.

Or are the dramatists playing with the audience's — lawyers! — ability to weigh evidence? We do not have much time to ponder the puzzlement; only twenty-three lines after he leaves the scene, his death is reported by Marcella, one of the queen's ladies-in-waiting; and her speech of praise for Porrex deserves the notoriety which Charles Lamb has given it. Lamb's belief that "Marcella obscurely intimates that the murdered prince Porrex and she had been lovers"[53] is extreme, but it indicates how Marcella's speech which contains information tinged with emotion affects a sensitive reader. Her account of the murder not only wrings pity for Porrex but causes us to recognize the unnatural maliciousness of that mother Videna who received some of our sympathy in the preceding scene:

> Is all the world
> Drowned in bloud and soncke in crueltie?
> If not in women mercy may be found,
> If not, alas! within the mothers brest
> To her owne childe, to her owne fleshe and bloud,
> If ruthe be banished thence, if pitie there
> May haue no place, if there no gently hart
> Do liue and dwell, where should we seeke it then?
> (IV, 2, 169-76)

The "mothers brest" brings to mind Videna's use of the image with a difference. How pitiful it all seems when we hear from Marcella that Porrex, already stabbed and bleeding, called to his mother for help, the very mother "whose direfull hand gave him the mortal wound."

With the cruel details of the murder behind her, with Gorboduc and Eubulus gone from the stage, Marcella lyrically evokes a picture of the prince that was:

> O queene of adamant, O marble brest,
> If not the fauour of his comely face,
> If not his princely chere and countenance,
> His valiant actiue armes, his manly brest,
> If not his faire and seemely personage,
> His noble limmes in such proportion cast
> As would have wrapt a sillie womans thought,
> If this mought not haue moued thy bloudy hart
> And that most cruell hand the wretched weapon
> Euen to let fall, and kiste him in the face,
> With teares for ruth to reaue such one by death, —
> Should nature yet consent to slay her sonne?
> O mother, thou to murder thus thy childe!
> Euen Ioue with iustice must with lightning flames
> From heauen send downe some strange reuenge on thee,
> Ah, noble prince, how oft haue I behelde
> Thee mounted on thy fierce and traumpling stede,
> Shining in armour bright before the tilt,
> And with thy mistresse sleue tied on thy helme,
> And charge thy staffe to please thy ladies eye,
> That bowed the head-peece of thy frendly foe!
> How oft in armes on horse to bend the mace!
> How oft in armes on foote to breake the sworde!
> Which neuer now these eyes may see againe.
> (IV,2,233-56)

The rhetorical repetitions and balances serve to heighten the emotion; the poetry is concrete and expressive. "As would have wrapt a sillie womans thought" is a line worthy of Shakespeare. Marcella's speech seems to tip the scales of pity in Porrex's favor, until, only ten lines later, the Chorus presents a stanza on Porrex's greedy lust for power, his wrath, his treason, and his cruelty — the qualities that attached to him before Marcella's praise. The Chorus's view of Porrex must be the one the dramatists hold, but Marcella's rhetorical and emotional indulgence — is she the "sillie woman"? — adds an interesting perspective to what could have been merely a cardboard character. The Chorus then discusses the Furies of the dumb show, emphasizing that "Blood aske blood, and death must death requite" — a commonplace already treated by Sackville in the *Complaint*.

Act IV testifies to the dramatists' effective control of audience response. The dumb show's pantomimic action, color, and music, followed by Videna's powerful soliloquy, raise the emotional temperature; the low-key trial scene, presenting balanced accusation and defense, reduces the temperature; and this scene is followed by the lyrically expressive and poignantly emotional speech by Marcella. The Chorus ends all with sententiousness and explanation. Since these emotional shifts work, this is one of the most theatrically effective acts in early English drama.

For most critics *Gorboduc* ends with Act IV; by Act V, the four main characters — Gorboduc, Videna, Ferrex, Porrex — are dead. But the play continues to display the results stemming from Gorboduc's division of the realm. Because of its clear statement of political principles, Act V seems to be the reason for the play's existence *and* the reason for the play's being criticized for lacking unity of action — "drawing out the plot beyond its due dramatic limits,"[54] a "postlude."[55] I contend, however, that "due dramatic limits" are set by the play itself, not by *a priori* standards; that the play shapes its own dramatic experience; that unity of action depends on what one considers to be the *center* of action; and that the absence of important characters cannot destroy a play's unity when no one character emerges as of the very highest importance and when the main characters appear on stage so few times. (Gorboduc appears three times, Videna twice, Ferrex and Porrex twice each but never together. Eubulus appears five times and is given more lines than any other character; he, after all, is speaking for the dramatists in a didactic play; his importance points to what should be the obvious focus in any discussion of the play's unity.)

Act V gracefully follows Act IV. It moralizes on the deaths of the protagonists and introduces an interesting new character, Fergus, whose attitude and action extend the play strictly in accordance with the dramatists' didactic purpose. In fact, the fifth act allows us to state with assurance that *Gorboduc* is the tragedy of a kingdom — as Willard Farnham indicates. At the same time he claims that the act violates dramatic unity.[56] The unity, I maintain, comes from our concern for Britain, which is a dramatic entity. The unity of Shakespeare's *Henry VI* plays is based on the same kind of premise.

The dumb show which precedes the controversial last act is

similar to the conventional battle scenes of many Elizabethan history plays. Armed men — not mythological or symbolic figures, but real men — march about the stage to the martial music of drums and flutes, and fire their weapons. This realistic action conveys the actual presence of chaotic civil war and is immediately recognizable as the present history of Britain — that is, a concrete representation not only of what the messengers will report *in the play,* but what the dramatists think will be the condition of England if Elizabeth does not listen to the words of Eubulus. The tumult of war is in the air, and the speeches of this act moralize this fact.

When the counselors meet, we learn that the people, provoked by the murder of Porrex, have slain "the giltlesse king" and the Queen. The people are rebellious, giddy, wavering, traitorous — the usual attitude toward the mob already expressed by Sackville in the *Complaint.* Their activity prompts Eubulus to deliver a long speech stressing a sense of urgency about the fate of Britain:

> Euen yet the life of Brittayne land doth hang
> In traitours balaunce of vnegall weight.
> Thinke not, my lordes, the death of Gorboduc,
> Nor yet Videnaes bloud will cease their rage.
> Euen our owne lyues, our wiues and children deare,
> Our countrey, dearest of all, in daunger standes
> Now to be spoiled, now, now, made desolate,
> And by our-selues a conquest to ensue.
> (V, 1, 58-65)

Here the dramatists are pointing directly at the chief protagonist of the play, "Our country, dearest of all." The repetitive "Now" highlights the immediacy of action necessary in both play and Elizabethan England. When the stage empties, one character remains to utter a Machiavellian soliloquy. Fergus, Duke of Albany, will take advantage of the confusion in the land and will seize power:

> If ever time to gaine a kingdome here
> Were offred man, now it is offred mee.

This is the "mee" of the self-centered opportunist filled with ambition; and, in this respect, he is an extension of Porrex, and a foreshadowing of Richard III in Shakespeare. The evil qualities in man emerge when no one strong ruler controls the land. Fergus succeeds in gathering an army of twenty thousand men. The forces of good, led by Eubulus, must now oppose the forces of evil as the "wretched land" is torn by civil war. Eubulus, in the course of uttering the important political sentiments discussed and quoted in a previous section, presents a movingly effective picture of the devastation of civil war:

> In the meane-while these ciuil armes shall rage;
> And thus a thousand mischiefes shall vnfolde,
> And farre and neare spread thee, O Britaine Land!
> All right and lawe shall cease; and he that had
> Nothing to-day, to-morrowe shall enioye
> Great heapes of golde, and he that flowed in wealth,
> Loe, he shall be bereft of life and all;
> And happiest he that then possesseth least.
> The wiues shall suffer rape, the maides defloured;
> And children fatherlesse shall weepe and waile;
> With fire and sworde thy natiue folke shall perishe;
> One kinsman shall bereaue an-others life;
> The father shall vnwitting slay the sonne;
> The sonne shall slay the sire, and know it not;
> Women and maides the cruell souldiers sword
> Shall perse to death; and sillie children, loe,
> That playing in the streetes and fieldes are found,
> By violent hand shall close their latter day!
> Whom shall the fierce and bloudy souldier
> Reserue to life? Whom shall he spare from death?
> Euen thou, O wretched mother, halfe aliue,
> Thou shalt beholde thy deare and onely childe
> Slaine with the sworde while he yet suckes thy brest.
> Loe, giltlesse bloud shall thus eche-where be shed!
> Thus shall the wasted soile yelde forth no fruite,
> But dearth and famine shall possesse the land!
> The townes shall be consumed and burnt with fire,
> The peopled cities shall waxe desolate;
> And thou, O Brittaine, whilome in renowme,
> Whilome in wealth and fame, shalt thus be torne,
> Dismembred thus, and thus be rent in twaine,
> Thus wasted and defaced, spoyled and destroyed!
> These be the fruites your ciuil warres will bring.
> (V,2,201-33)

The speech, by means of concrete examples, makes vivid the chaos — children playing in the streets; a baby at his mother's breast. The father-son killings will be presented *on stage* when Shakespeare wants to dramatize his picture of civil war in the *Henry VI* plays. The mother-child references call to mind that mother Videna who had two children at her breast, but who slaughtered one child. Underlying all is the deeply felt sorrow of Eubulus for "thou, O Brittaine." After so devastating a speech, the last four lines of the play, expressing hope for restoration, seem weak:

> Yet must God in fine restore
> This noble crowne vnto the lawfull heire;
> For right will alwayes liue and rise at length,
> But wrong can neuer take deepe roote, to last.
> (V,2,276-79)

All will be left in the hands of God. It is difficult to be certain of the intent of these lines. Are they the genuine expression of hope in a providential movement of history? Are they the easy sentiments that we associate with the other advisers in the play? Do we think now of the other optimistic references to the gods which immediately were undercut by the events in the play? Can four lines of hope make up for one hundred lines of woe? I suspect that the students of the first audience saw these last lines as a token gesture, but then again history did unfold, and at the moment of viewing, "right" *is* living in the person of a Queen Elizabeth who, hopefully, will heed the good advice given her.

I have attempted to demonstrate, by means of a running commentary, that *Gorboduc* is stageworthy. Although disparaged by all critics as a piece of theater, the play was intended originally for the stage only; printing it was forced upon Sackville and Norton. It is true that the burden of the play is thrown on rhetorical language, that the play is academic; but we must not discount the totality of the play's effect — that is, the balanced rhetorical intellectual set speeches exist *with* speeches that are emotional, poignant, and sometimes moving and *with* dumb shows that are colorful, spectacular, symbolic. The statement of the play exists *with* the story and *with* the action of the dumb show. All three cooperate to one explicit end, which is moral and political.

The play's action is unified. It is based on a tight cause and effect structure. This story of crime and punishment proceeds in an orderly consequential fashion; the revenge theme informs the sequence of events. (This, I have suggested, is probably Seneca's most important contribution to Elizabethan drama.) And all events affect the main focus of the action, Britain. The various motifs — revenge, ambition, family dissension, civil dissension, advice, flattery — are directly related to that central character England in a play that is relentlessly political and didactic.

The play does not contain highly individualistic characters because the characters exist for their didactic effects. The advisers, including Eubulus, are points of view, not flesh and blood. Ferrex is merely a good son and prince. Porrex seems merely evil — although the shifting perspective on him suggests a complexity not possessed by the other characters. Fergus is a prototype of the ambitious opportunist. Videna, however, is a powerful creation, evoking both compassion and abhorrence. She is a loving mother filled with tenderness for a son, and she is an unnatural mother filled with hatred for another son. She has good motives for her action, but her act is hideous. She is the only character in *Gorboduc* whose dramatic function clings wholly to the emotional rather than the didactic. Gorboduc, the titular hero, is a good man and just king. His actions are well-meaning, but his single foolish act of dividing his land results in his own suffering and death and in the destruction of his kingdom. That he is a good man has important implications for the development of tragedy, which is discussed in the final chapter; but his character has little dimension.

At times, *Gorboduc* displays genuine poetry of a high order, as we would expect from the author of the "Induction" and the *Complaint.* All the speeches in the play are rhetorical; they are built on balanced patterns, contain formal diction, and appeal to ears that expect the mechanical harmonies. Good rhetoric is usually not good poetry, but the dramatists manage to make much of their rhetoric easy-flowing, melodious, and, most important to tragedy, moving. Videna's soliloquy, Marcella's praise of Porrex, scattered lines that resound, and strong choric comments stand out as fine poetry by sixteenth-century standards and by our own. That the poetry is often effective without the help of metaphor is interesting, since metaphor is an important feature of Elizabethan drama. However, the play does contain the kind of image motif we associate with Shakespeare — imagery of fire relating to strife in family and nation, animal imagery indicating the unnatural forces of disorder, and the Phaethon image highlighting the theme of rebellion and pride and the fall of princes.

By means of the many references to "gods" and to "death," the dramatists create the atmosphere of tragedy. The allusions to

Classical mythology and the invocations to the gods — including two to "God" — establish a "high" ground for the working out of the tragic plot. The sheer number of references to "death," more than twice as many as in *King Lear,*[57] establish the climate of doom, as do the third and fourth dumb shows.

The structure, characters. language and atmosphere of the play all relate to the single objective of teaching a political lesson. The didactic aim, however, does not diminish the theatrical nature of the play; for the dramatists have succeeded in effectively juxtaposing the dumb shows and the rhetorical speeches, the pantomimic action and the verbal non-action, the spectacle and the word. *Gorboduc* has a secure place in the history of English drama — the first "regular" tragedy, the first chronicle history play, the first play in blank verse — but it can stand on its intrinsic qualities as a stageworthy work of art.

CHAPTER 7

Thomas Sackville and Elizabethan Tragedy

THOMAS Sackville is the victim of "the most perfect conspiracy of approval," to use T. S. Eliot's phrase in his notorious essay about Ben Jonson. Praised for having written the best poem between Chaucer and Spenser, lauded for having presented a play to which the word "first" is always attached, Sackville is read only by historians, antiquarians, and students studying for doctoral comprehensives. My preceding chapters on the "Induction," the *Complaint,* and *Gorboduc* have attempted to demonstrate that these works have intrinsic merit and that Thomas Sackville is a fine literary artist as well as a name in literary histories.

Although we must return inevitably to Sackville's well-preserved niche in the history of English literature, the quick enumeration of "firsts" and the fleeting comments of praise do not adequately suggest Sackville's rich contribution to the development of Elizabethan tragedy. To know Thomas Sackville — to know his two poems and one play — is to know where Elizabethan tragedy came from and where it was going.

Perhaps the most famous definition of tragedy in the Middle Ages is given by Chaucer's Monk:

> Tragedie is to seyn a certeyn storie,
> As olde bookes maken us memorie,
> Of hym that stood in greet prosperitee,
> And is yfallen out of heigh degree
> Into myserie, and endeth wrecchedly.

The Monk attributes to Fortune this fall from prosperity; but when Lydgate relates his tales in *The Fall of Princes,* he attributes the fall from high degree to vices in the fallen men, illustrating not merely the turning of capricious Fortune's wheel but the punishment of sinners by God. The most important descendant of Lydgate's *Fall of Princes* was, as we have seen, *The Mirror for Magistrates,* where the falls of famous men of British history were recounted. The *Mirror* gave to Elizabethan drama the dramatic material it would use — for it provided an inexhaustible mine for tragical stories — and it popularized the notion that a high man falls because of Fortune, *â la* Chaucer, or because of his own guilt, *â la* Lydgate, or both.[1]

Sackville's *Complaint* confronts the important question of tragic responsibility in a way that directly anticipates later Elizabethan tragedy. As my discussion of the poem in Chapter 5 has indicated, Sackville fuses the ideas of Fortune, individual responsibility, and God's justice; he makes the Duke of Buckingham responsible for his own actions which cause him to become a slave of Fortune and which lead to his fall and death. At the same, Sackville surrounds this fusion with an air of mystery (the constant use of the question), emphasizes the idea of mutability, and propels the narrative by means of the revenge theme. Throughout, the Duke of Buckingham has a *dramatic* presence. A ghost, soliloquizing, presents his story with fine detail and appropriate gesture, emotionally responds to his own narration, and displays a guilty conscience and a sensitive soul. He is a sympathetic sinner who realizes his villainy, wishes to amend his life, but is compelled to follow an ever-narrowing course with fewer and fewer choices to his destruction. Sackville clearly exposes Buckingham's inner nature and allows his depiction of Richard III and Banaster to expand to a generalization about man's self-seeking nature, his treachery, ambition, and the fragility of his affections.

In this tragical narrative, therefore, Sackville brought to Elizabethan tragedy one approach to the complexity of tragic responsibility — a tragic character who errs but is sympathetic — and a reflection on man's evil nature; he uses revenge as an important motivating force; and, with Sackville's use of the interrogative, he suggests the mysteriousness that surrounds all tragic worlds, just as with his emphasis on blood and death he infuses the poem with a powerful sense of man's vulnerability and mortality. If any one narrative in *The Mirror for Magistrates* clearly points to the greatness of Elizabethan drama, Sackville's *Complaint* must be the one.

The "Induction," not a tragical narrative in the strict sense, contains fewer tragic ingredients that can be imitated in the later drama.

The poem presents ideas found in later tragedies — the fall of princes, Fortune, the theme of mutability; but these, as we have seen, seem less important than the poem's atmosphere. The atmosphere, however, is one of tragedy. Sackville's picture of winter evokes a dark tragic world, for winter is described as an inevitable force devastating the natural world. The summer that was is replaced by the winter that is. The "was" and "is" progression in nature leads to a contemplation of the same sequence in fallen princes, in tragic heroes. The landscape of tragedy is presented with no relief. Contemplating the inevitable changes in the seasons could lead to the comforting conclusion that winter too ends in favor of spring; but Sackville allows for no such thought. His change is to winter — and nothing follows. The fact of death and its finality give the poem its special tragic power — a quality noticed, we can assume, by the Elizabethan dramatists who read the popular "Induction."

The poem's allegorical personages belong to a poetic world rather than to a dramatic one, but they represent some aspects of human behavior — Conscience, Revenge, Death, War — which will give Elizabethan tragedy its distinctive flavor and which the writers in the morality tradition have already used in drama. The poet's journey to the underworld is an epic device, but even here the atmosphere that Sackville evokes is closer to Elizabethan tragedy than to Classical epic. Sackville offers no relief to the darkening gloom; his journey displays neither Virgil's hopes nor Dante's doctrine. Nor does his description contain the slightest echo of the reassuring Harrowing of Hell, the very popular episode in the mystery cycles. Only the terror and the sorrow of the journey are emphasized — the density of the air, the feeling of constriction, the sheer unrelieved devastation of the condition of those in hell. An epic device, it is charged with a tragic atmosphere — just as that epic happening, the fall of Troy, becomes the epitome of tragedy for the Renaissance mind.

Important elements of later Elizabethan tragedy are present in the poems — the fall of high men, the working of Fortune and God's justice, notions of tragic responsibility, the evil impulses of man, the atmosphere of mortality — but in *Gorboduc* these are found in a work *written for the stage*. Consequently, *Gorboduc* makes the more direct contribution to the development of Elizabethan tragedy.

In Chapter 6, I have discussed the specific ways in which *Gorboduc* combines elements of the native tradition with those of the Senecan tradition. But it bears repeating that the fusion of the two traditions in *Gorboduc* is itself an important contribution to

Elizabethan drama. The play is attached to the popular tragic tradition of the tragical narratives in the *Mirror for Magistrates* — a logical attachment in the light of Sackville's contributions to the *Mirror* — and it displays specific aspects of the morality plays. It goes directly to the chronicles on British history for its source material, thereby establishing itself as the first chronicle history play and indicating to future English playwrights the rich dramatic sources available to them in their own nation's past (which the non-dramatic narratives of the *Mirror* also indicated). Sackville raises the history play to a more formal and artistic level when he turns to Seneca. Seneca helps to make *Gorboduc* the first "regular" tragedy — with its five-act structure, precise balances, sense of decorum — and, more important, as I have indicated, it probably suggested to Sackville how the revenge theme could shape the course of a play's action, giving it a tight structure, a cohesion based on cause and effect. In *Gorboduc,* two potent traditions meet and join, the Renaissance wedding a happy one for the future of the drama.

The exact nature of tragic responsibility in *Gorboduc* has far-reaching effects on Elizabethan tragedy. We noticed that, in the *Complaint,* Buckingham's evil actions led to his downfall, with Fortune and God's justice parts of the overall scheme. In *Gorboduc,* the downfall of the king is also caused by his own behavior, but his intentions are good; that is, unlike Buckingham, Gorboduc must be considered an essentially good man who committed an error of judgment. We must agree with S. F. Johnson's fine observation that the political purpose of the play forced the dramatists to present Gorboduc as a good monarch, for Queen Elizabeth was meant to identify with Gorboduc. Because Elizabeth was not an evil ruler and could not be expected to relate to an evil one, Sackville and Norton had to avoid the conventional *Mirror* view of tragedy as the fall of an evil man.

Moreover, Sackville and Norton had to avoid an over-emphasis on the capricious aspects of Fortune because they were interested in teaching a political lesson based on avoidable, tragic consequences of human actions. The play does contain passages explaining the fall of Gorboduc in terms of predestination (fate, curse, Trojan line) and in terms of Fortune, but these cancel each other out in favor of a picture of the tragic fall of a virtuous man whose punishment far exceeds his crime. Gorboduc's initial act of dividing his land — stemming, I repeat, from good motives — releases forces that make his fall a certainty. Although the act itself was avoidable — and, therefore, an implied lesson to Elizabeth — once it was done, the consequences were inevitable. For the first time in English drama we find that a single well-meaning, but unwise, act of a high man can release in others forces that are inherently evil, impulses that are anarchic and egocentric — usually ambition and revenge — and can begin an irreversible chain of events leading to death and chaos. *Othello* and *King Lear* do not seem too far off in the future.

Gorboduc, therefore, gives to Elizabethan tragedy the pattern for a specific kind of tragic progression. In addition, Sackville and Norton offer a tragic insight — inadvertently, I think, because their specific didactic purpose seems to have pushed them to their unconscious achievement — that cuts through the form and the rhetoric to say something important about the human condition, which all tragedies must do. In *Gorboduc,* a central paradox of Elizabethan tragedy is presented, although not explored, that good and evil, the virtuous and the chaotic, are somehow dependent upon each other.

Interestingly, Gorboduc is a prototype for future virtuous tragic heroes without himself taking center stage in his own play. I have indicated that, in *Gorboduc,* we have the tragedy of a kingdom; but in the play various characters (Gorboduc being the most important to the plot and to the kingdom) are presented separately, each having a turn as the center of attention. The total action focuses on Britain, and each character plays a role in pushing the nation closer to the horror of civil war. Most important in the play, and most important to its didactic purpose, is the effect of the mistakes and crimes on the nation as a whole. The suffering of individuals becomes less significant than that of the state, which is presented so effectively by Eubulus in the last big speech of the play.

This tragic perspective has a greater effect on later Elizabethan chronicle history than on Elizabethan tragedy: for the latter stresses the suffering of the individual whose actions usually affect the state; the former, the suffering of the state itself. There is little doubt, for example, that Shakespeare had *Gorboduc* in mind when he wrote his *Henry VI* plays and *Richard II.* The Bishop of Carlisle's prophetic speech in *Richard II* asserting that "The blood of English shall manure the ground,/ And future ages groan for this foul act" contains strong echos of Eubulus' speech. Among many other calamities, Shakespeare in *2 Henry VI* also dramatizes one of the fruits of civil war that Eubulus presents:

> The father shall unwitting slay the sonne;
> The sonne shall slay the sire and know it not.

Shakespeare gives the image a visual dimension and symbolic significance that far transcends the original statement in *Gorboduc* but that definitely recalls and relies on the original. Even the larger pattern in *Gorboduc* of a realm left vulnerable to civil war and to the ambitions of power because a sure heir is not known has much in common with Shakespeare's histories. In short, *Gorboduc* as the tragedy of a nation is closer to the Elizabethan history play than to the Elizabethan tragedy; but the individuals causing the tragedy of a state, especially the good king Gorboduc, belong to Elizabethan tragedy.

By its very nature, a tragedy of state evokes more tragic fear than tragic pity. The reader of *Gorboduc* has little opportunity to be moved by pity for any of the characters. Gorboduc's "weake despaire" and lack of any sense of his own guilt diminishes whatever pity we may feel for him. Videna's cruelty and her unnatural crime work against whatever warm feeling we may have for her tender relationship with her older son. Marcella's elegy, which evokes some pity for Porrex, is undercut immediately by the Chorus. Porrex himself is never emotional in his grief, never even histrionic in his trial scene. Pity, therefore, is not effectively excited in *Gorboduc*. Fear, on the other hand, is stressed — for the audiences at the initial performances of *Gorboduc* were meant to fear for their own future and safety. The emphasis on blood and chaos, the waste of civil war, the afflictions of all people, the piteous spectacles reported in speeches and seen in dumb shows — all play on fear to bring home the play's message. The dramatists' didactic purpose, therefore, informs not only the particular quality of tragic hero but the particular kind of tragic emotion felt by the audience. In the *Complaint*, Sackville effectively evoked tragic pity for Buckingham and surely was capable of doing the same for any of the characters in *Gorboduc;* in *Gorboduc,* he correctly realized that fear was the more potent weapon in a propagandizing play.

The tragic potentialities of *Gorboduc* that I have been discussing, those aspects of the play that seem to point directly to the Elizabethan tragedy of the future, can be discerned more clearly, perhaps, by briefly comparing *Gorboduc* — to its disadvantage, of course — to *King Lear.* The basic similarities are obvious: in each play an aged king of legendary British history divides his land against the advice of good counselors, unleashes human impulses that are evil, and causes family and nation to suffer tragically. Beyond this similarity we find in Shakespeare, as we do in Sackville and Norton, an emphasis on the terrible consequences that arise when the natural restraints of family and government are withheld. We find in both *Gorboduc* and *King Lear* that the king's initial action lacked any trace of evil design; but, nonetheless, each unleashed forces of evil, latent ambitions and hatreds, that eventually destroy the commonwealth. In both plays the tragic atmosphere pervades — with pagan deities, heavens, and God evoked; with blood flowing thickly; with death always present. In both the action is precipitous, one event quickly following another to its inevitable tragic conclusion. At the end of both an expression of hope is sounded, and in each this expression seems muted in the context of horror and chaos.[2]

To explore these similarities more closely is to see why *Gorboduc* is at the beginning of a development, not to mention why Shakespeare is the greater dramatist. In *Gorboduc,* the events are related by speeches alone; the play's action is found in the dumb shows but does not stem directly from the play's events; the play lacks the visual effect of a Kent in the stocks, or a naked Tom o' Bedlam leading a blind Gloucester, or a mad Lear in weeds. In *King Lear,* the king who makes a mistake suffers so greatly that he evokes tragic pity; he has a sense of his own guilt; and he acquires new values on his pilgrimage toward death. In Shakespeare's tragedy, we are concerned with the individual more than with the state, although they are bound together. The entire action centers on Lear, with even the Gloucester underplot commenting on and relating to the Lear story; in *Gorboduc,* the action centers on the state, making the play less personal, less able to evoke pity. In *King Lear,* the characters are invested with a human dimension that the characters in *Gorboduc* lack. Shakespeare's play carries a symbolism and an atmosphere that leads to reflections about the world in general. At times, by presenting the ambitious and revengeful impulses of man, by invoking the gods, *Gorboduc* touches this higher dimension, but the chaos that comes seems local when compared with the universal destruction, "the promised end," of Lear's world.

Comparing the plays in this way — a foolish comparison if we wish merely to demonstrate Shakespeare's superiority — is useful in suggesting that *Gorboduc* was a praiseworthy stimulus to the poetic imagination of Shakespeare. It deserves its epithet "the first English tragedy" not only because of its accomplishment — a striking accomplishment, if we compare *Gorboduc* not to *King Lear* but to the other Inns of Court tragedies and to such popular tragedies as *Cambises* — but because it provided some of the conditions which eventually produced great tragedy.

The most important condition, discussed in Chapter 6, must now be reaffirmed — the introduction of blank verse to drama. For Elizabethan tragedy to flourish, a verse form had to be developed which was exactly suited to the purposes and effects of tragedy. The choice of blank verse seems natural to us, with its great practitioners behind us. But blank verse was not the medium for an acted play before Sackville and Norton used it in *Gorboduc,* thereby making the first English tragedy the first play to use blank verse — a fortunate coincidence for the future of Elizabethan tragedy. A tragic hero is what he is able to express; a tragic action is controlled by the words of the play's characters; the quality of tragic paradoxes and mysteries depends on the way words give them shape. T. S. Eliot places this accomplishment of Sackville and Norton in its proper perspective when he states that blank verse is "the instrument without which the Elizabethan drama would have been impossible."[3]

Thomas Sackville's importance to the development of Elizabethan tragedy can hardly be overestimated. As a true Renaissance man, he presented in his poems and play the fusions and conditions, the materials, that make great tragedy possible. The spark to ignite these materials came three decades later with Kyd and Marlowe, and the fire blazed with Shakespeare and the Jacobean dramatists.

Notes and References

Chapter One

1. The details of Sackville's life are based chiefly on: *Dictionary of National Biography,* ed. Sidney Lee (London, 1885-1900); Marguerite Hearsey, *The Complaint of Henry, Duke of Buckingham* (New Haven, 1936); Jacobus Swart, *Thomas Sackville, A Study in Sixteenth Century Poetry* (Groningen, 1948); Paul Bacquet, *Thomas Sackville, L'Homme et L'Oeuvre* (Geneva, 1966).

2. *The English Works of Roger Ascham,* ed. James Bennet (London, 1761), pp. 193-94.

3. George Abbot, *A Sermon preached at Westminister, May 26, 1608* (London, 1608), p. 13.

4. *The Book of the Courtier,* ed. Walter Raleigh (London, 1900), p. 4.

5. Sir Robert Naunton, *Fragmenta Regalia* (pr. 1641), *The Harleian Miscellany* (London, 1809), II, 103-04.

6. The document is reprinted in full in Swart, p. 10.

7. F. W. Maitland presents interesting details on Sackville's Roman affair in "Thomas Sackville's Message from Rome," *The English Historical Review* (October, 1900), 757-60.

8. Quoted in Swart, p. 6.

9. J. B. Black, *The Reign of Elizabeth* (Oxford, 1936), p. 116.

10. Sir Winston Churchill, *A History of the English Speaking Peoples* (New York, 1960), II, 108.

11. Swart, p. 19.

12. Quoted in Hearsey, pp. 34-35.

13. J. A. Froude, *The Reign of Elizabeth* (London, 1932), III, 348.

14. Quoted in Hearsey, p. 35.

15. Quoted in Swart, p. 21.

16. Sackville's mission to the Netherlands is treated in great detail and appraised in glowing terms by John L. Motley, *History of the United Netherlands* (New York, 1861), II, 213-59, 277-80.

17. Quoted in Swart, p. 17.

18. Recorded in V. Sackville-West, *Knole and the Sackvilles* (London, 1923), p. 35.

19. A thorough discussion of Sackville's religious beliefs can be found in Bacquet, pp. 102-8.

20. Abbot, *Sermon,* p. 18.
21. Preamble of the will of Thomas Sackville, in R. W. Sackville-West, *The Works of Thomas Sackville* (London, 1859), p. xlvi.

Chapter Two

1. George Turberville, *Tragical Tales and other Poems* (Edinburgh, 1837), p. 11.
2. C. Gregory Smith, *Elizabethan Critical Essays* (Oxford, 1904), II, 327.
3. *Du Bartas, His Devine Weekes and Works,* trans. Joshua Sylvester (London, 1608), p. 211.
4. *The Poetical Works of Edmund Spenser* (Oxford, 1912), p. 412.
5. George Saintsbury, *A History of Elizabethan Criticism* (London, 1887), p. 11.
6. Professor Campbell's edition, *The Mirror for Magistrates* (New York, 1960), will be used throughout.
7. Willard Farnham, "The Progeny of *A Mirror for Magistrates,*" *Modern Philology,* XXIX (1932), 395.
8. It is the relentless moral comment that has proved most repellent to modern readers, most of whom would agree with James Russell Lowell that the *Mirror* is the "most dolefully dreary of books." *Harper's Magazine,* LXXXV (1892), 195.
9. Thomas Warton, *History of English Poetry* (London, 1824), IV, 33, 36.
10. Joseph Haslewood, ed., *Mirror for Magistrates* (London, 1815).
11. W. J. Courthope, *History of English Poetry* (London, 1897).
12. J. W. Cunliffe, *The Cambridge History of English Literature* (Cambridge, 1910), V.
13. W. F. Trench, *A Mirror for Magistrates: its Origin and Influence* (Edinburgh, 1898).
14. Fitzroy Pyle, "Thomas Sackville and *A Mirror for Magistrates,*" *Review of English Studies,* XIV (July, 1938), 315-21.
15. Swart, pp. 33-38.
16. Pyle believes it was written before 1557; Bacquet before 1563.

Chapter Three

1. H. O. White, *Plagiarism and Imitation During the English Renaissance* (Cambridge, Mass., 1935), p. 202.
2. Hardin Craig, "The Shackling of Accidents: A Study of Elizabethan Tragedy," *Philological Quarterly,* XIX (January, 1940), 23.
3. For a detailed discussion of Sackville's sources, see Bacquet, pp. 177-198.
4. Swart, p. 53.
5. Elizabeth Nitchie, *Vergil and the English Poets* (New York, 1966), p. 95.

6. *The Poetical Works,* vol. III, Book VI, Chap. 4, ll. 7-11, 17.
7. This borrowing is specifically noted by both Swart, p. 49, and Douglas Bush, *Mythology and the Renaissance Tradition in English Poetry* (Minneapolis, 1932), p. 63. W. W. Skeat considers the stanza "one of the finest stanzas in our language." *Specimens of English Literature* (Oxford, 1917), p. 466.
8. G.L. Kittredge, *American Journal of Philosophy,* IX (1888), 84-85.
9. Bacquet, p. 187.
10. Swart, p. 56.
11. See Hearsey, p. 116, for specific quotations from Valerius Maximus.
12. This parallel is cited by Hearsey, p. 108.
13. *Hall's Chronicle* (London, 1809), p. 395.
14. Specific discussion of these ballads is found in Swart, pp. 60-61.

Chapter Four

1. C.S. Lewis, *English Literature in the Sixteenth Century* (Oxford, 1954), pp. 244, 325-26.
2. Close discussion of the verse and style can be found in the following: Bacquet, pp. 281-302; Swart, pp. 99-120; D. A. Davie, "Sixteenth Century Poetry and the Common Reader: The Case of Thomas Sackville," *Essays in Criticism,* IV (1954), 117-27; V. L. Rubel, *Poetic Diction in the English Renaissance* (New York, 1941), pp. 165-71. Swart and Rubel emphasize the rhetorical devices; Davie stresses syntax; Bacquet's discussion includes all aspects of verse and style.
3. Lewis, p. 325.
4. See Swart, pp. 117-19, and Bacquet, pp. 281-82, for specific discussion of archaisms.
5. Swart, pp. 92-93; Rubel, pp. 165-71.
6. E. M. W. Tillyard, *The Elizabethan World Picture* (London, 1956), pp. 48-55.
7. Herbert J. C. Grierson and J. C. Smith, *A Critical History of English Poetry* (New York, 1946), p. 71.

Chapter Five

1. Grierson and Smith, p. 71.
2. Donald Davie is the only critic who considers the *Complaint* the better poem.
3. Willard Farnham, *The Medieval Heritage of Elizabethan Tragedy* (Berkeley, 1936), p. 293.
4. R. G. Howarth, "Thomas Sackville and *A Mirror for Magistrates,*" *English Studies in Africa,* VI (March, 1963), 90.
5. Bacquet, p. 124.
6. Howard Baker, *Induction to Tragedy* (New York, 1939), p. 208.
7. I am indebted to D. W. Robertson, Jr. for his convincing explanation

of the concept of Fortune. "Chaucerian Tragedy," *English Literary History,* XIX (1952), 1-37.

Chapter Six

1. Homer A. Watt, *Gorboduc; or Ferrex and Porrex* (Madison, 1910), p. 7.
2. David Daiches, *A Critical History of English Literature* (New York, 1960), I, 223.
3. Sir Philip Sidney, *An Apologie for Poetry* (1595), in G. Gregory Smith, I, 196.
4. Quoted in Watt, pp. 12-13.
5. Charles Lamb, *Specimens of English Dramatic Poets* (London, 1808), p. 5.
6. *The Diary of Henry Machyn,* ed. John G. Nichols (London, 1848), p. 275.
7. The facts on Thomas Norton's life are extracted from Sidney Lee's account in the *Dictionary of National Biography.*
8. Warton, IV, 195.
9. A detailed discussion of these internal differences is beyond the scope of this study. Bacquet, pp. 230-47, presents an analysis of the problem and reviews the findings of previous scholars.
10. See L. H. Courtney, "Tragedy of *Ferrex and Porrex," Notes and Queries,* ser. II, X (1860), 262; and Baker, p. 28. For an excellent account of the early parliamentary situation in Elizabeth's reign, see Sir John Neale, *Elizabeth and Parliament, 1559-1581* (London, 1953).
11. Discussions of the play's political ideas can be found in Watt, pp. 33-45; Swart, pp. 71-74; Baker, pp. 18-29; Bacquet, pp. 127-49; and in the following articles: Courtney, pp. 261-63; Sarah R. Watson, "*Gorboduc* and the Theory of Tyrannicide," *Modern Language Review,* XXXIV (1939), 355-66; S. A. Small, "The Political Import of the Norton Half of *Gorboduc," Publications of the Modern Language Association,* XLVI (1931), 641-46; Gertrude C. Reese, "The Question of Succession in Elizabethan Drama," *University of Texas Studies in English* (1942), 59-85; Ernest W. Talbert, "The Political Import of the First Two Audiences of *Gorboduc,"* in *Studies in Honor of DeWitt T. Starnes* (Austin, 1967), 89-115; David Bevington, *Tudor Drama and Politics* (Cambridge, Mass., 1968), 141-47.
12. The text of *Gorboduc* used throughout is found in *Chief Pre-Shakespearean Dramas,* ed. Joseph Quincy Adams (New York, 1924), pp. 503-35, which is based on the second edition (1570) in the British Museum. A fine edition of the play in modern spelling, prepared by Irby B. Cauthen, Jr., was published by the University of Nebraska Press in 1970.
13. The motif of "good advice" is examined in Small's article.
14. Swart, p. 72.
15. Talbert, p. 89.

16. Courtney, p. 261.
17. S. F. Johnson discusses this important idea in his unpublished Harvard dissertation, *Early Elizabethan Tragedies of the Inns of Court* (1948), pp. 543-55, and in his article, "The Tragic Hero in Early Elizabethan Drama," in *Studies in English Renaissance Drama*, eds. J. W. Bennett, O. Cargill, V. Hall, Jr. (New York, 1959), 157-71.
18. Watt, p. 53.
19. Swart, p. 69.
20. Bacquet, pp. 218-24.
21. Two scholars who are strong in their belief that Sackville and Norton went to the Senecan Theban story are: A. W. Ward, *A History of English Dramatic Literature* (London, 1899), I, 200; Felix E. Schelling, *The English Chronicle Play* (New York, 1902), p. 20.
22. H. Schmidt, "Seneca's Influence Upon *Gorboduc*," *Modern Language Notes*, II (1887), 56-70.
23. John W. Cunliffe, *The Influence of Seneca on Elizabethan Tragedy* (London, 1893).
24. Felix E. Schelling, *Elizabethan Drama, 1558-1642* (Boston, 1908).
25. F. L. Lucas, *Seneca and Elizabethan Tragedy* (Cambridge, 1922).
26. T. S. Eliot, *Selected Essays* (New York, 1932), pp. 51-88.
27. Watt, pp. 54-73.
28. Baker, pp. 30-47.
29. *Ibid.*, p. 34.
30. Farnham, *Medieval Heritage*, p. 354.
31. Marvin T. Herrick, "Senecan Influence in *Gorboduc*," in *Studies in Speech and Drama in Honor of Alexander M. Drummond* (Ithaca, 1944), 78-104.
32. Henry W. Wells, "Senecan Influence on Elizabethan Tragedy: A Re-Estimation," *Shakespeare Association Bulletin*, XIX (1944), 71-84.
33. Bacquet, pp. 249-68.
34. Wells, p. 84.
35. In this I am in full accord with Bacquet, p. 259.
36. Two works that convincingly discuss Seneca's contribution to the structure of Elizabethan drama are: H. E. Fansler, *The Evolution of Technic in Elizabethan Tragedy* (Chicago, 1914); Madeleine Doran, *Endeavors of Art* (Madison, 1954).
37. The importance of this scheme, especially of the tavern phase, to the development of Elizabethan drama is discussed in the present writer's *The Base String: The Underworld in Elizabethan Drama* (Rutherford, N. J., 1968).
38. Bacquet, p. 267.
39. Baker, p. 32.
40. Watt, pp. 76-77.
41. John W. Cunliffe, "Italian Prototypes of the Masque and Dumb

Show," *Publications of the Modern Language Association,* XXII (1907), 140-56.

42. Fine discussions of the origin of dumb shows can be found in George Kernodle, *From Art to Theatre* (Chicago, 1944); and Dieter Mehl, *The Elizabethan Dumb Show* (London, 1965).

43. T. S. Eliot, p. 82.

44. Baker, p. 68.

45. Providing "perfect proof of continuity" in the work of poets of the sixteenth century, as Baker suggests, pp. 63-68. See also Baker's "Some Blank Verse Written by Thomas Norton before *Gorboduc,*" *Modern Language Notes,* XLVIII (1933), 529-30.

46. Watt, p. 83.

47. Wolfgang Clemen, *English Tragedy before Shakespeare* (London, 1961), p. 65.

48. John Bakeless, *The Tragicall History of Christopher Marlowe* (Cambridge, Mass., 1942), II, 178.

49. S. F. Johnson, pp. 696-764.

50. See Baker, pp. 58-59.

51. Moody Prior presents an excellent discussion of the evolution of blank verse in *The Language of Tragedy* (New York, 1947).

52. Clemen, p. 73.

53. Lamb, p. 10.

54. J. A. Symonds, *Shakspere's Predecessors in the English Drama* (London, 1884), p. 232.

55. Edmund Creeth, intro. to *Tudor Plays* (New York, 1966), p. xxxix.

56. Farnham, *Medieval Heritage,* p. 353. That the commonwealth is protagonist is also recognized by Baker, pp. 39-40, and Irving Ribner, *The English History Play in the Age of Shakespeare* (Princeton, 1957), p. 45.

57. See Barbara H. C. De Mendonca, "The Influence of *Gorboduc* on *King Lear,*" *Shakespeare Survey,* XIII (1960), 41-48, for a comparison of the two plays.

Chapter Seven

1. The problem of tragic responsibility in the *Mirror* is discussed by William Peery, "Tragic Retribution in the 1559 *Mirror for Magistrates,*" *Studies in Philology,* XLVI (1949), 113-30.

2. For more specific comparisons, see Barbara H. C. De Mendonca, pp. 41-48.

3. T. S. Eliot, p. 82.

Selected Bibliography

PRIMARY SOURCES

The Mirror for Magistrates, ed. Lily B. Campbell. New York: Barnes and Noble, 1960. The best edition of this important collection of tragical narratives, containing Sackville's "Induction" and *Complaint*. Professor Campbell's sixty-page introduction discusses the book's genesis and contents with clarity and thoroughness.

The Complaint of Henry, Duke of Buckingham, ed. Marguerite Hearsey. New Haven: Yale University Press, 1936. A fine edition of the autograph manuscript which presents the "Induction" and the *Complaint* as a single poem. Includes the unfinished Epilogue.

Chief Pre-Shakespearean Dramas, ed. Joseph Quincy Adams. New York: Houghton Mifflin, 1924. Contains the second and authorized edition (1570) of *Gorboduc*.

Gorboduc; or, Ferrex and Porrex, ed. Irby B. Cauthen, Jr. Lincoln: University of Nebraska Press, 1970. A modern-spelling edition of the play.

SECONDARY SOURCES

BACQUET, PAUL. *Thomas Sackville, L'Homme et L'Oeuvre*. Geneva: Libraire Droz, 1966. Thorough, authoritative, full-length French biography and critical study.

BAKER, HOWARD. *Induction to Tragedy*. Baton Rouge: Louisiana State University Press, 1939. Contains valuable discussions of Sackville's poems and *Gorboduc*.

CLEMEN, WOLFGANG. *English Tragedy before Shakespeare*. London: Methuen, 1961. Includes a fine examination of *Gorboduc* as a rhetorical tragedy.

COURTNEY, L.H. "Tragedy of *Ferrex and Porrex*," *Notes and Queries*, Series II, X (1860), 261-63. The first scholar to discuss the relationship of the political speeches in *Gorboduc* to the political events of the time.

CRAIG, HARDIN. "The Shackling of Accidents: A Study of Elizabethan Tragedy," *Philological Quarterly*, XIX (1940), 1-19. Informative account of Seneca's influence on Elizabethan tragedy, especially Shakespeare.

CUNLIFFE, JOHN W. *The Influence of Seneca on Elizabethan Tragedy.* London: Macmillan, 1893. Influential discussion of Seneca's influence on *Gorboduc.*

DAVIE, D. A. "Sixteenth Century Poetry and the Common Reader: The Case of Thomas Sackville," *Essays in Criticism,* IV (1954), 117-27. Perceptive examination of Sackville's syntax.

DE MENDONCA, BARBARA H. C. "The Influence of *Gorboduc* on *King Lear,*" *Shakespeare Survey,* XIII (1960), 41-48. Indicates the many similarities between the two plays.

DORAN, MADELEINE. *Endeavors of Art.* Madison: University of Wisconsin Press, 1954. Valuable study of almost every aspect of Elizabethan drama, including Senecan influence.

ELIOT, T. S. *Selected Essays.* New York: Harcourt, Brace, 1932. Contains the essay entitled "Seneca in Elizabethan Translation," a discussion of the English translations of Seneca found in Thomas Newton's edition of *Seneca His Tenne Tragedies* (1581). Eliot stresses the importance of blank verse to the development of Elizabethan drama.

FANSLER, H. E. *The Evolution of Technic in Elizabethan Tragedy.* Chicago: Row, Peterson, 1914. Contains a good discussion of Seneca's influence on the structure of Elizabethan tragedy.

FARNHAM, WILLARD. *The Medieval Heritage of Elizabethan Tragedy.* Berkeley: University of California Press, 1936. Indispensable to an understanding of the native tradition, including *The Mirror for Magistrates,* as it affects the nature of Elizabethan tragedy.

HERRICK, MARVIN T. "Senecan Influence in *Gorboduc,*" *Studies in Speech and Drama in Honor of Alexander M. Drummond.* Ithaca: Cornell University Press, 1944. Intelligent, balanced discussion of Senecan influence in *Gorboduc,* indicating that the play is Senecan, but not "merely Senecan."

JOHNSON, S. F. "Early Elizabethan Tragedies of the Inns of Court." Unpublished doctoral dissertation, Harvard University, 1948. Contains an informative, perceptive discussion of *Gorboduc.*

— — — "The Tragic Hero in Elizabethan Drama." *Studies in the English Renaissance Drama.* New York: New York University Press, 1959. Argues convincingly that Gorboduc is a prototype for later Elizabethan tragic heroes.

KERNODLE, GEORGE, R. *From Art to Theatre.* Chicago: University of Chicago Press, 1944. Discusses the origin of the dumb show and its importance to Elizabethan drama.

LEWIS, C. S. *English Literature in the Sixteenth Century.* Oxford: Oxford University Press, 1954. Contains discussions of the tragical narratives in *The Mirror for Magistrates,* including Sackville's poems.

LUCAS, F. L. *Seneca and Elizabethan Tragedy.* Cambridge: Cambridge

University Press, 1922. Includes a good discussion of Seneca's influence on *Gorboduc.*

MEHL, DIETER. *The Elizabethan Dumb Show.* London: Methuen, 1965. Thorough examination of the origins and contents of dumb shows.

NITCHIE, ELIZABETH. *Vergil and the English Poets.* New York: AMS Press, 1966. Discusses Virgil as a source for the "Induction."

PRIOR, MOODY. *The Language of Tragedy.* New York: Columbia University Press, 1947. Includes a fine discussion of the development of blank verse in English drama.

PYLE, FITZROY. "Thomas Sackville and *A Mirror for Magistrates,*" *Review of English Studies,* XIV (1938), 315-21. Discusses the printing of the "Induction" and the *Complaint,* making the interesting suggestion that Baldwin edited the poems during the course of printing.

REESE, GERTRUDE C. "The Question of Succession in Elizabethan Drama," *University of Texas Studies in English* (1942), 59-85. Discusses the important implications of the political speeches in *Gorboduc.*

RIBNER, IRVING. *The English History Play in the Age of Shakespeare.* Princeton: Princeton University Press, 1957. Contains a discussion of *Gorboduc* as history play and tragedy.

ROBERTSON, D. W., JR. "Chaucerian Tragedy," *Journal of English Literary History, XIX* (1952), 1-37. Excellent disscussion of the concept of Fortune.

RUBEL, V. L. *Poetic Diction in the English Renaissance.* New York: Modern Language Association of America, 1941. Contains an examination of Sackville's use of rhetorical devices.

SCHMIDT, H. "Seneca's Influence upon *Gorboduc,*" *Modern Language Notes,* II (1887), 56-70. First scholar to discuss Seneca's influence on *Gorboduc.*

SMALL, S.A. "The Political Import of the Norton Half of *Gorboduc,*" *Publications of the Modern Language Association,* XLVI (1931), 641-46. Good discussion of the play's political ideas.

SWART, JACOBUS. *Thomas Sackville, A Study in Sixteenth-Century Poetry.* Groningen: J. B. Wolters, 1948. Presenting materials for an historical appreciation of Sackville's work, this study argues convincingly on the importance of rhetoric to the Elizabethan poetic tradition.

TALBERT, ERNEST W. "The Political Import of the First Two Audiences of *Gorboduc.*" *Studies in Honor of DeWitt T. Starnes.* Austin: University of Texas Press, 1967. Careful, convincing discussion of the political background to *Gorboduc.*

WATSON, SARAH R. "*Gorboduc* and the Theory of Tyrannicide," *Modern Language Review,* XXXIV (1939), 355-66. Discusses the contemporary political situation as it relates to *Gorboduc.*

WATT, HOMER. *Gorboduc; or, Ferrex and Porrex.* Madison: Bulletin of the University of Wisconsin, 1910. Examines *Gorboduc* as a "mirror" for seeing contemporary influences and conditions.

WELLS, HENRY W. "Senecan Influence on Elizabethan Tragedy: A Re-Estimation," *Shakespeare Association Bulletin,* XIX (1944), 71-84. Fine refutation of the findings of previous commentators on Seneca's influence on Elizabethan tragedy.

Index

Abbot, George, 14
Allde, Edward, 82
Ascham, Roger, 14, 101

Bacon, Francis, 17, 21
Bacquet, Paul, 29, 31, 39, 44, 76, 91, 95, 99
Baker, Howard, 76, 93, 94, 95, 99, 101
Baldwin, William, 26, 27, 28, 30, 31, 44
Blenerhasset, Thomas, 26
Boccaccio, 25, 26, 27, 32
Boethius, 33, 77, 96
Boleyn, Anne, 13
Boleyn, William, 13
Burghley, Lord, 17, 20

Calvin, John, 83, 101
Cambises, 97
Campbell, Lily B., 25, 29, 30
Campion, Thomas, 24
Castiglione, 15
Castle of Perseveraunce, 39
Catherine de Medicis, 17
Charles IX, 17
Chaucer, Geoffrey, 32, 33, 36, 37, 39, 44, 45, 77, 99, 120
Cheke, John, 101, 102
Churchill, Winston, 18
Cicero, 97
Clemen, Wolfgang, 111
Courthope, W. J., 29
Courtney, L. H., 90
Craig, Hardin, 32
Cranmer, Archbishop, 83
Cunliffe, J. W., 29, 93, 94, 95, 100

Daiches, David, 80
Daniel, Samuel, 53
Dante, 48, 50, 51, 122
Day, John, 82, 83
Devereaux, Robert, 21, 22
Dictes or Sayings of the Philosophers, 32
Douglas, Gawain, 35, 37
Dryden, John, 81
Du Bartas, 24

Edward VI, 13
Eliot, T. S., 93, 101, 120, 127
Elizabeth I, 13, 14, 16, 17, 18, 19, 20, 77, 81, 85, 86, 87, 99, 100, 101, 102, 107, 115, 117, 123, 124
Essex, Earl of, *see* Devereaux, Robert
Everyman, 39

Fabyan, Robert, 26, 42, 43, 91, 92
Farnham, Willard, 27, 76, 94, 114
Fletcher, John, 103
Froude, J. A., 20

Gardiner, Stephen, 26
Geoffrey of Monmouth, 91, 92
Goodman, Christopher, 88
Grafton, Richard, 91, 92
Grey, Catherine, 85, 87
Griffith, William, 82
Grimald, Nicholas, 101, 102

Hall, Edward, 26, 42, 43, 62, 64, 69, 75
Hardyng, John, 92
Haslewood, Joseph, 29
Hearsey, Marguerite, 29, 30, 60
Herrick, Marvin, 94
Higden, Ranulf, 92
Higgins, John, 26
Hoby, Thomas, 15
Homer, 51

Howarth, R. G., 76

Ippolito de Medici, 101

James I, 17
Johnson, S. F., 90, 102, 123
Jonson, Ben, 120

Kittredge, G. L., 39
Kyd, Thomas, 127

Lamb, Charles, 81, 112
Lee, Sidney, 29
Leicester, Earl of, 18, 20
Lewis, C. S., 44, 45
Lucan, 24
Lucas, F. L., 93
Lydgate, John, 25, 26, 36, 37, 39, 40, 41
 68, 82, 99, 120, 121

Machyn, Henry, 81
Marlowe, Christopher, 102, 103, 127
Mary (Stuart), 22, 85, 87
Mary (Tudor), 13
Maximianus, 39
Mirror for Magistrates, 21, 24-31, 37, 49,
 52, 66, 76, 82, 83, 93, 99, 110, 121, 123
More, Thomas, 26, 42, 64

Niccols, Richard, 29
Nitchie, Elizabeth, 33
Norton, Thomas, 17, 80-119 *passim,* 123,
 126, 127

Ovid, 32, 36

Philip II of Spain, 87
Plutarch, 36, 40
Pope, Alexander, 81
Pyle, Fitzroy, 30

Respublica, 98
Rubel, V. L., 45
Rymer, Thomas, 81

Saintsbury, George, 25, 44
Sackville, Richard, 13, 14
Sackville, Thomas,
 WORKS:
 Complaint of Henry, Duke of Buckingham, 13, 15, 17, 26, 30, 31, 32, 33, 36, 39-43, 44, 55, 59, 60-79, 114, 115, 118, 121, 123, 125
 Gorboduc, 13, 15, 17, 18, 30, 31, 80-119, 122, 124, 125, 126, 127
 "Induction," 13, 15, 17, 23, 26, 28, 30, 31, 33-39, 43, 44-59, 60, 61, 62, 69, 71, 76, 78, 96, 118, 121, 122
Sackville-West, R. W., 29
Sackville-West, V. M., 29
Schelling, Felix, 93
Schmidt, H., 93
Seneca, 32, 33, 35, 37, 39, 43, 66, 92-98,
 99, 101, 102, 117, 123
Shakespeare, William, 43, 53, 64, 65, 69,
 75, 76, 102, 103, 111, 114, 115, 116,
 117, 118, 119, 124, 125, 126, 127
Sidney, Philip, 45, 53, 80, 81, 93, 96, 102
Spenser, Edmund, 24, 25, 33, 44, 120
Surrey, Earl of, 30, 32, 35, 37, 39, 40,
 101, 102
Swart, Jacobus, 18, 28, 31, 33, 39, 45, 90,
 91
Sylvester, Joshua, 24

Talbert, Ernest, 90
Terence, 94
Tottel's Miscellany, 30, 101
Trench, W. F., 30
Trissino, Giovanni, 101
Turberville, George, 24

Valerius Maximus, 36, 40
Virgil, 32, 33, 34, 35, 36, 37, 39, 43, 50,
 51, 101, 122

Walsingham, Francis, 18
Warton, Thomas, 25, 29, 83, 84
Watson, Sara, 88
Watt, Homer, 80, 91, 93, 99
Wayland, John, 26
Wells, Henry W., 94, 95
Whitchurch, Edward, 83
Wyatt, Thomas, 32, 37